# Rise From Your Ashes

## *Memoir of a Woman Who Found Beauty in Her Brokenness*

Brittany Jenkins

RISE FROM YOUR ASHES

RISE FROM YOUR ASHES

*Memoir Of A Woman Who Found Beauty In Her Brokenness*



This is a work of nonfiction. The events, experiences, and reflections contained within these pages are true to the author's recollection and perspective. Some names and identifying details have been changed to protect the privacy of individuals mentioned.



**ISBN:** 979-8-9954454-0-1

**Cover & Interior Design:** Olaiya Tolu-Jacobs
**Editor:** Olaiya Tolu-Jacobs
**Published by:** Beauty in Healing LLC *(Self-Published Imprint)*

For speaking inquiries, bulk orders, or permissions:
www.IamBrittanyJenkins.com
hello@iambrittanyjenkins.com

*First Edition, 2026*

*To my late Husband.*
*The laughter that still lingers,*
*The love time cannot erase.*
*You were the echo in every page of this healing.*
*This is for you.*

# CONTENTS

# PREFACE

Let me tell you how this book even happened. I was in my apartment (in the living room) watching TV. Nothing special. And out of nowhere, this thought dropped into my spirit. Not a random idea; a full *download*. A book. Not just my story, but space for *your* story too. Reflection woven in. Something to walk with you, not just talk at you.

I was so excited. It felt so clear, so real. I started writing, no clue what I was doing, no outline, no plan. Just this stirring I couldn't ignore.

Funny thing? People had been telling me since I was a teenager that I'd write a book someday. I'd laugh. *Me? A book? Nah.* I never saw myself as an author. Never thought my messy life was worth the pages. Books were for people who had it all together, right? Not someone still surviving.

But maybe that's exactly why this matters.

It's about the falling apart and choosing to breathe anyway. Diagnosis. Disappointment. Death. Grace in the grief. Questions when God feels quiet; and finding out He was there all along.

I wrote this with whispered prayers, tears in the dark, clinging to verses like Romans 8:28 when they felt like the only thing keeping me afloat.

I used to think ashes meant it was over. You know that feeling, when something burns up, you just assume it's done. Finished. Nothing left worth saving. But here's what I've learned in the fire: ashes aren't the end. They're proof something made it through.

This book is not some deep theology lesson. It's just my story of making it through. A reminder that healing can start even when you're still broken. I didn't write because I felt ready or worthy. I wrote because something in me *knew* I had to.

If your life feels like ashes right now, this book is for you. There's beauty coming, even if you can't see it yet. And if God can use my ashes to hold space for yours, then every hard thing was worth it.

This is my story.

But I hope it feels like yours, too.

Rise with me.

**Brittany Jenkins**

Founder,

*Beauty in Healing*

# ACKNOWLEDGEMENT

There are not enough words to capture the gratitude I carry, but I will try. **Dar-Lynn and Lorenzo Jenkins**, my mom and dad, were my first example of real strength. Through every dark season, they stood with me, prayed over me, and held me up. My sisters, **Tiffany, Tanisha, and Tempestt**, have been my anchor when the waves felt relentless. Their support was spiritual, emotional, and unconditional. Special love to my nieces and nephews: **Mylani, Makiyah, Micah, Malachi, and Aston.** You may not have known it, but you saved me in those early months. Pouring into you gave me a reason to show up when grief had made me feel invisible. To my editor, **Olaiya:** your insight and patience helped shape this into something I am genuinely proud of. Above all, none of this happens without **God.** When I begged Him to let me go, He tightened His grip. Word by word, day by day, He spoke beauty over my brokenness until this book became possible. **This is His story. He just trusted me to tell it.**

*There were nights I begged God to take my life. No, I didn't want to die. I just didn't want to feel the pain anymore. But even there. In the fire. In the silence. In the breaking. God came. He didn't rescue me from the ashes.* ***He restored me through them.***

# INTRODUCTION

**I am not perfect.**

I did not write this book from a mountaintop. I wrote it from the valley. From the aching, bewildering experience of a woman who loved deeply, lost profoundly, and somehow, by the tenacious grace of God, found her way through the fire. I am Brittany Jenkins: therapist, widow, daughter, dreamer, and a woman who has had to learn — more than once — how to rise.

If you are holding these pages, some part of your story has brought you here. Maybe you are grieving something you cannot name. Maybe you have been strong so long you have forgotten what it feels like to simply be held. I want you to know: I have stood in that same place. And I know, not as a theory but as a testimony, that what feels like an ending can become the most unexpected beginning.

There is no map for suffering. No rulebook for rising. This memoir began in pain, but it does not belong to the pain. It is a love letter to the possibility of beauty; the kind that does not arrive *after* the devastation, but takes root *inside* it.

My twenties were wide open, luminous, full of certainty. I entered my thirties newlywed, full of plans, convinced I was writing the best chapter yet. Then a diagnosis arrived (a rare blood disorder), and the future narrowed overnight to the width of a hospital corridor. Before I found my footing, both of my parents were hospitalized in the same season. Then came the long ache of a cross-continental marriage, immigration delays that stretched longing into years, and the quiet grief of miscarriage.

Nothing, though, prepared me for what came next.

My husband was in Ghana, in the final stages of our visa process, when something shifted in the atmosphere around him. I felt it before I could name it. I even dreamed of his death. When my phone rang before dawn with the words *he is gone*, time stopped being a reliable thing. No training, no faith I had built, no resilience I had gathered could blunt the raw edge of it. In those long, dark nights, I begged God to let me go to sleep and not wake up — not because I wanted to die, but because I did not know how to keep waking up inside that much pain. I say that plainly because I believe someone reading this needs to know you can feel that and still be found.

And I was found.

Not instantly. Not in a blaze of relief. But in the softest, most persistent way, a presence that did not explain itself but simply refused to leave. Restoration came not as an event, but as a direction: *this way. Slowly. One morning at a time.*

What I learned is this: the way forward is not *around* the ashes. It is *through* them. This book is not a prescription for suffering well, nor a triumph narrative. I am still becoming, still healing. It is, simply and deeply, the story of what God can do with ashes… and an invitation for you to let Him do the same with yours.

# BEFORE YOU BEGIN

For a long time, I was not sure the world needed to hear my story. Sharing yourself publicly when you are naturally a private person is a kind of courage that does not always feel brave in the moment. It mostly just feels terrifying.

But the Lord has a way of reminding you that your story was never, really, just yours. So, if you are here, holding these pages, I do not think that is an accident. I believe you are connected to something in this story that God wants to use to speak to your own.

As you move through each chapter, I have created three spaces just for you:

1. **Self-Reflection:** Honest questions to help you pay attention to what is stirring inside you as you read. No assessments. No wrong answers. Write your responses here in the book or scan the QR code to reflect digitally.
2. **Speak This Over Yourself:** A short declaration of truth to help you begin speaking life over yourself, especially on the days when the weight of your season feels heavier than your hope. Read it quietly. Speak it aloud. There is power in what we confess over our lives.
3. **Let's Pray:** A prayer to close each chapter: simple, honest, and written from one healing heart to another. For the moments when you want to bring your story before God but aren't quite sure where to begin.

You are allowed to go at whatever pace your heart needs. Some chapters will pass through you easily. Others will find something tender and ask you to stay a little longer. Let them.

# *Rise From Your Ashes*

# I
# THE GIRL BEFORE THE FIRE

*"Before I formed you in the womb I knew you,*
*before you were born I set you apart."*
*– Jeremiah 1:5 (NIV)*

Before the fires ever came, before grief sang its slow, sorrowful ballad and pain rewrote my path, there was a time I soaked in joy.

Now, with the clarity that only hindsight brings, I see it all: simple, shining mornings; laughter refracting off kitchen counters; and the soft rhythm of sneakers gliding across worn blacktop.

There was bliss. There was freedom. There was Long Island, New York—my beginning, my home, the place where my roots ran deep and my journey quietly began. Long Island was more than a location; it was a heartbeat. Saturdays smelled like fresh bagels. Streets buzzed with familiar footsteps and front-porch conversations. Neighbors greeted each other like long-lost family. In the summer, you could hear the hum of lawnmowers.

In the fall, the crack of school doors opening. In the evening, the joy of families celebrating birthdays in their backyards.

Our small neighborhood on the Island was a tight-knit community where everyone knew everyone. It was the kind of place where people knew your name, your background, and what court you played on after school. From kindergarten to high school, my classmates were constant companions. We witnessed each other's growth in a small-town school system where everyone knew everyone, from childhood to senior year.

Summers brought adventure. From trips to Sesame Place to long drives to South Carolina to visit my dad's family, childhood was joyfully ordinary. It was laughter at cookouts, tightly knit family bonds, and the kind of memories that seem small when you're living them, but sacred when you look back.

Sesame Place felt magical. Nestled in Pennsylvania, it was a water park and Sesame Street fantasy rolled into one bright, colorful world where childhood came alive. Elmo and Big Bird felt like real-life friends. Laughter filled the splash zones, and even now I can still hear the sound of it in my memory. My sisters and I would race through winding water slides, chase bubbles in the lazy river, and wave at our favorite characters in the parade as if they would wave back.

Then there were the road trips: Long Island to South Carolina, a yearly pilgrimage back to my dad's roots. Those long car rides were filled with snacks, music, and sibling silliness. Stories traveled between my sisters in the back seat while the highway stretched endlessly ahead. We would arrive to the embrace of extended family and the warm hugs of cousins we only saw once a year. The house always smelled like cake and comfort. Those visits were more than family gatherings; they were reminders of where our story began, of the heritage that shaped us. As the years passed and our lives took us in different directions, those gatherings became less frequent. I still miss the closeness and carefree joy we shared in those days.

I was the last daughter of four girls, trailing behind my older sisters by six, eight, and twelve years. The baby. The gap child. But never forgotten. I was cherished and coached. I was raised in a household full of love, laughter, and the constant rhythm of bouncing basketballs. We were a sports family—all of us. But basketball? Basketball was mine.

My dad was my coach and my champion. He introduced me to the game when I was only five years old. Basketball quickly became more than a sport; it became identity. It became the bond between my dad and me, the thread running through summer tournaments, long practices, and memories made across state lines.

In high school, I was the girl with the game. Known. Celebrated. Respected. I played point guard and shooting guard. I was the floor general. I called the shots. I set the pace. I was the one my teammates looked to when the clock was winding down. Even then, before I fully understood it, I was learning how to lead and how to carry the weight of other people's expectations.

But losing was a different kind of weight.

Every missed shot felt personal. Every loss felt like I had let down my coach, my dad, my whole team. The pressure to perform, to win, to be perfect—it was constant. From the outside, people saw the medals, the celebrations, the wins. What they didn't see was the knot in my chest when I didn't meet expectations, the self-blame, the voice inside whispering, you're not enough.

Looking back now, I can call it what it was: anxiety.

At the time, I didn't have the language. I didn't know how to say I was drowning in pressure while still smiling for photos. I just kept pushing. Kept showing up. Kept proving. What I didn't realize was that basketball wasn't only building my body; it was building my backbone. It was preparing me for the griefs, the losses, and the silent storms I had not yet met.

There was also another pressure quietly rising beneath the surface: expectation.

In my family, basketball had already carved a path before me. My sisters had earned college scholarships to play, and when my turn came, I wanted to continue that legacy. I wanted the opportunity they had. I wanted to prove that the line did not end with me. But as senior year drew closer and the scholarship process became more uncertain, anxiety followed me there too. For the first time, I had to wrestle with the possibility that the future I had imagined might not unfold the way I had planned.

Around that same time—when I was waiting for a scholarship and hoping to continue the family basketball legacy—a family friend called me with a word that, in hindsight, I now understand was both promise and warning. It came about a week or two before I went to visit a school and meet with coaches, hoping for an opportunity to earn a spot on the team and receive a scholarship. She told me I would get the scholarship. But she also told me to be careful when I got there, because there was someone I might connect with who could be used to derail what God was trying to do in my life.

At the time, I heard the blessing more clearly than I heard the warning.

I was so focused on the open door that I did not fully grasp the caution attached to it. I wanted the dream. I wanted the opportunity. I wanted the scholarship. And for a moment, it seemed like everything was falling into place.

But when I got to college, the person I had been warned to avoid became one of the very first people I connected with. I was strangely pulled toward her. The friendship felt easy at first. Familiar. Harmless. But over time it led me into spiritual confusion and pain I never anticipated. That season eventually spiraled into a depressive episode that resulted in me being admitted to a psychiatric hospital for a few days. It also altered the course of my college basketball career in ways I never imagined.

I did not continue to play at that first school.

In my second year, I transferred to another school and started playing basketball again. I could have continued, but there were deeper issues with the school itself. It was struggling financially, and it was not the kind of environment where I could truly build a future. After my first semester there, I made the decision to go back to New York, move home with my parents, and transfer to Adelphi University.

By then, the dream I once thought would carry me through college—basketball—could no longer pay the price of the journey. But the Lord did not allow that loss to derail my life or cancel His purpose for me. What I lost on one path, I had to fight for on another.

There was also a pattern in my family I had become deeply aware of: not finishing school, not finishing higher degrees, not seeing the journey all the way through. Somewhere along the line, I made up my mind that the pattern would end with me. Even when basketball was no longer the vehicle I had counted on, I found another way. Through academics, through scholarships, through perseverance, I kept going.

I graduated from Malverne High School in 2009, and it felt like a triumph, but nothing quite compared to the moment I walked across the stage at Adelphi University in 2014, bachelor's degree in social work in hand. A year later, in 2015, I added my Master's to that legacy.

Malverne was where I first learned to carry pressure. It was where Friday nights buzzed with basketball games, cheering classmates, and the electric pulse of being known. It was where I learned to push through fear and embrace friendships that felt unbreakable.

Adelphi, though, became something different. It was the place where I discovered my passion for social work. It was the place where a life bigger than basketball began to take shape. Adelphi helped form me into a woman ready to face the world beyond courts, trophies, and familiar streets.

Against every odd that whispered otherwise, I became the first in my family to earn a college degree. I went on to become a licensed clinical social worker, a title forged not just in classrooms, but in the fire of every moment I nearly gave up. It was never just my victory. It was ours. It was for us. It was for my whole family. It was for every unfinished story that came before mine.

I was achieving on paper. I was also becoming. I was learning how to stand on my own, exploring life outside my family's familiar orbit. I traveled the world solo—to Italy, to Bali, to Mexico—chasing sunsets and healing pieces of myself I didn't yet know were broken. I had once been ruled by anxiety, paralyzed by fear and judgment. But the road gave me wings. Freedom gave me permission.

Solo travel became therapy. I was not just seeing the world; I was meeting myself. I began to discover what I liked and what I did not. I began to say yes to life. I realized fear no longer had the final word over me. By then, I understood that the courage I was growing into had started long before—in the church, through my mother, and in my early relationship with Jesus.

My mother was the one who first introduced me to church, to Christianity, and to Christ.

As a little girl, I did not always understand it. I felt out of place most Sundays in Sunday school because the other children seemed to know so much more than I did. Most of them had been immersed in church from the beginning, while I only went when my mom took me. Because of that, I gave her a lot of pushback over the years. Even so, the Lord was still after my heart. He did not interpret my resistance as rejection, and He never stopped drawing me to Himself.

That continued into my early teens, when I gave my life to Christ. Later, around eighteen or nineteen, I chose to be baptized. But even after that, my faith was still growing. I wanted to follow God, but I was still learning what that actually looked like. The trials I faced in high school and college were not God punishing me; they were the consequences of my own choices and decisions. I had convictions, but I did not yet have the full revelation of who He was or how deeply He loved me.

And still, He was with me.

So much so that He tried to warn me before I ever got to college. Looking back, I can see that His hand was on my life even in the seasons I did not fully understand. He was already speaking, already preparing me, already trying to guard me from what was ahead. I just did not yet have the maturity to fully recognize what He was saying.

That adds another layer to the story of my relationship with God, because it shows how He kept revealing Himself to me over time. As I grew older and walked through different seasons, my understanding of Him grew too. What I can see now is that His presence was never missing. His right hand was over my life all along.

God was, truly, present all along, even when I did not fully see it for myself. He was speaking, guiding, and trying to prepare me long before I had the maturity to recognize His voice.

Still, in that season—before the heartbreaks, before the losses—I was thriving. I had purpose. I had dreams. But I had no idea how much I would one day need the strength I was building.

This was the woman before the ashes. Whole. Hopeful. On fire for life.

But fire has a way of testing everything you think you are.

And soon…

Mine would begin to burn.

# Self-Reflection

1. What part of my story most spoke to your own?

2. How would you describe your own "before the fire" season; the time before life became heavy?

3. Were there any early warning signs in your story that you ignored? Why do you think you did?

4. What was a passion, activity, or dream that gave you purpose in your early years?

5. Can you remember a time when anxiety or fear had a grip on your identity? What helped you through it?

6. Do you believe your past prepared you for what you're facing today? Why or why not?

7. What part of your childhood or early adulthood would you like to reclaim or revisit with fresh eyes?

***Want to go deeper with your reflection?*** *After you complete this chapter's journal prompts, you can choose to share your answers privately with me. With your consent, your story may be included anonymously in a future devotional sequel.*

## NOTES

..... / .... / ......

S M T W T F S

*Before you move on, what else did God stir in you through this chapter?*

SPEAK THIS OVER YOURSELF

# My past is not wasted. My pain is not pointless. My God is still writing my story.

**Dear God,**

*Thank You for the version of me that existed before the fire; the hopeful, carefree, bold, or even broken version of me who was still growing. Help me to honor that part of my story, not with shame or regret, but with compassion. Reveal the moments You were preparing me, even when I didn't know it. Help me to see that nothing I've walked through is wasted. Remind me that You were there then, and You are here now.* ***In Jesus's name. Amen.***

# II
# ASHES IN MY BLOOD

*"So do not fear, for I am with you..."*
*– Isaiah 41:10 (NIV)*

I used to believe that transformation came with some kind of announcement. A trumpet. A burning bush you simply could not miss. But the Lord has a way of moving quietly – slipping into the ordinary spaces of your life and rearranging everything while you're still busy making plans.

People ask me sometimes, "*Brittany, when did everything change?*" And every time, I find myself reaching back through memory, turning things over, searching for one clean moment I can hand them. But that's not really how life works, is it? Life unfolds layer by layer, and most of the time we don't recognize the turning point until we're already standing on the other side of it. Still, if I had to draw a line somewhere, I'd draw it in 2019.

That unpredictable, tumultuous year of 2019.

Four years out of graduate school, I had settled into the kind of life I'd worked hard to build. It wasn't perfect (nothing ever truly is) but it was mine, and I was genuinely grateful for it. My career had purpose. My relationships had roots. And my heart was full. I had just traveled to Ghana, drawn by a longing to experience the continent of Africa, to immerse myself in its culture, its people, its beauty. It was meant to be nothing more than that. But the trip held a surprise I never saw coming: a deep and unexpected connection with someone who would later become my husband.

We weren't yet married, but we were already weaving our futures together across oceans and time zones, exchanging faith and possibility like love letters written in hope. Life felt like it was finally, truly opening up.

I had no idea that a single year would reach in and strip away the simple joys I had taken for granted. That year became the boundary between then and now; the border where my spiritual warfare began.

I returned from Ghana with my heart full and my future taking shape. What I didn't know was that I was stepping back into a world already standing on the edge of something none of us (no nation, no hospital, no family) could have prepared for. COVID-19 crept in the way a rumor does — quietly at first, then all at once.

I was working at a hospital in Queens, New York, immersed in the kind of purposeful labor I had trained hard for. And I was one of the first at my hospital to be exposed. It didn't arrive gently. The aching bones, the low fever, the pounding headache, the fatigue, the loss of taste, the loss of smell — they all came at the same time. All at once, like a wave that doesn't give you a moment to brace yourself. I called out sick for a couple of days and listened to what my body was telling me. I thought I was recovering.

I rested as I was told to do and allowed my body to recover. After a few days, I felt well enough to return to work. But the taste and smell never came back.

Not for a week. Not for a month. For an entire year. Now, I know that might not sound like a big deal. But try eating your favorite meal and tasting nothing. Try it for 365 days. It was, to put it plainly, annoying.

And yet, strangely, I didn't spiral. I didn't panic. I shrugged it off the way you do when a doctor looks you in the eye and says, '*It's normal. It's just the virus.*' So I believed them. I kept moving. I went about my days – cooking meals I couldn't taste, stepping outside into air I couldn't smell, noticing that the rare moments something did register, it tasted like nothing at all, or worse, like bleach. But the doctors had an answer, and so I held onto that answer like it was enough. I told myself I was fine. And for a long time, I almost believed it.

That summer, I went in for my routine checkup – the same one I had been doing every year since I turned 18 at the same PCP office. The process never changed. Blood draw. A prick. A waiting game. Then a phone call a few days later telling me everything looked fine. I had no reason to expect anything different this time.

The nurse greeted me the way she always did. We exchanged the usual pleasantries. I rolled up my sleeve without a second thought, watched the vial fill, and went on with my day. A few days later, the results came back.

I was at work when I got the news. Something in my blood had raised its hand and refused to be ignored.

There was a protein. An M-Spike.

I remember sitting there at my work computer preparing to wrap things up for the day, the result fresh in my hand, my heart already picking up speed. I turned to one of my co-workers – someone I trusted, someone who understood the language of labs and results the way I did – and I said quietly, "Hey, can I talk to you for a second? I'm a little nervous." I showed her what I was looking at. I told her there was a protein in my blood that the result was flagging as a possible indication of some type of cancer.

She looked it over and reassured me, the way only someone in healthcare can – calm, measured, grounded. She said that sometimes these things do show up, but that more often than not, they turn out to be nothing serious. That I shouldn't draw any conclusions before following up with my doctor. That I should wait.

My PCP referred me to a hematologist-oncologist – a word that, even just hearing it, carried a weight I wasn't quite ready to sit with. What struck me was that this wasn't entirely new territory. I had visited this same specialist once before, back in my early teens, when there had been a mild concern about slight anemia. They had brushed it off as nothing major then, sent me on my way, and life had continued without a second thought. I had hoped this would be the same.

Every six months, I returned – not just to that specialist's office, but across oceans. I found myself traveling back and forth between Ghana and New York, carrying the weight of unanswered questions with me on every flight. Each visit was its own quiet exercise in patience – sitting in that familiar office after crossing time zones to get there, waiting for answers, hoping the numbers would finally tell a different story. The same blood work. The same waiting game. The working theory at the time was that the COVID antibodies still lingering in my system could be the source of the M-Spike. A possibility. A maybe. Something to monitor rather than act on.

Sometimes the levels had stayed exactly the same. Sometimes they crept up slightly, just enough to tighten something in my chest that I refused to name. And then there were the visits where the numbers dipped, even just a little, and in those moments, hope would bloom quietly. I would leave the office walking a little lighter, allowing myself to believe, just maybe, that the tide was turning. But visit after visit, month after month, the protein remained – stubborn and unmoved, refusing to disappear completely the way we had all been quietly, collectively hoping it would. It had become an uninvited guest that no one knew how to ask to leave.

I held onto the idea that COVID was to blame. It was the most hopeful explanation on the table. I came back again and again, hoping the next round of tests would confirm it. *It's just a fluke,* I told myself. *Like the trace of anemia I had as a teenager. It will clear.*

The numbers didn't move.

The endless cycle of tests, blood draws, results, follow-ups, and conversations about what this protein in my blood could possibly mean had taken a toll I hadn't fully accounted for. Somewhere in the middle of all of it, I developed what doctors call white coat syndrome – a very real, very physical anxiety response triggered simply by walking into a medical setting. My blood pressure would rise the moment I sat down in that office. Not because something new was wrong, but because my nervous system had learned to brace for bad news before anyone even spoke.

Or maybe it wasn't only fear. Maybe it was also hope, the particular kind of hope that sits quietly in your chest on the drive over, whispering, *maybe this time.* Maybe this time I would walk in and the numbers would tell a different story. Maybe this time the doctor would look up from the chart with a soft smile and say, '*It's gone. The protein is gone. Your numbers are back to normal.*' That was what I wanted… so deeply.

Every appointment became its own quiet battle before it even began. I would sit in that waiting room and turn the tools of my trade on myself – breathing slowly, in for four counts, out for six, the same rhythm I walk my therapy clients through when their world feels like it's closing in. I was willing my body to listen. Trying to convince my own heart that it was safe to be still.

If my blood pressure read too high, it would raise a new concern entirely. The doctors would wonder whether I was developing hypertension, whether I needed medication, whether there was yet another thing to monitor and manage. I was fighting to keep one problem from creating another, and would do it all quietly, in the cold air of the waiting room, before my name was even called.

After a year and a half of back-and-forth visits, of watching the numbers hold stubbornly in place and the M-Spike refuse to budge, my hematologist determined that we had monitored long enough. It was time for the next step. Time to stop watching and start searching, to finally try to put a name to the mystery that had been quietly living in my blood. He ordered a bone marrow biopsy, sometime in the latter months of 2020.

But I didn't go right away.

I kept putting it off. Every time I thought about making the call, something in me found a reason to wait just a little longer. Another week. Another month. I wanted so badly for this not to be my reality that I did what many of us do when reality feels too heavy to face — I deferred. And then deferred again. I stretched the timeline as far as I possibly could, right up until the referral was on the verge of expiring and I had run out of road to delay on.

In therapy, we have a name for this. We call it avoidance; a very human, very understandable response to anything that feels painful, frightening, or potentially life-altering. I had sat across from clients and gently named this pattern in them. And here I was, living it fully, hoping that if I waited long enough, the need for the answer might somehow disappear along with the question.

Deep down, beneath all the deferring and the hoping and the quiet bargaining, I knew. I knew it had to be done. I knew that whatever was happening silently inside my body deserved a name — and that I deserved to know it.

Only then did I finally go. That was February 2021.

I want to be honest with you: I had built the biopsy up in my mind into something terrifying. Having someone drive a long, sharp needle into your bone to draw out plasma is every bit as painful and frightening as it sounds. But the experience itself was quieter than I expected. I was under anesthesia. I didn't feel a thing. And in one of life's quiet ironies, the moment I had spent months dreading turned out to be the one where I felt complete peace. Under anesthesia, I simply did not know, and for that brief window, not knowing was its own kind of mercy.

I just remember speaking briefly with the doctor and the nurse before they put me under and then being gently woken up on the other side. My sister came and picked me up. They sent me home with a little lunch. I went on about the rest of my day as though nothing had happened, no pain, no drama, just a return to my regular routine. But I knew the results were coming.

And that waiting was its own kind of weight. A week or so later, I went back to my hematologist for the results.

I remember sitting down on the little bed in the exam room across from the doctor. The room felt smaller than usual. He had the report in front of him – detailed, clinical, several pages long – and he walked me through it carefully, the way doctors do when they are trying to make sure you are following, when they are trying to make sure the weight of what they are saying lands slowly enough not to shatter you.

The abnormal protein was still there. Present in a minimal amount, but present. Confirmed. Undeniable.

He looked at me and said it plainly: *Brittany, you have what we call MGUS.*

He explained that the protein in my blood was what they called an M-spike, a marker for a condition my mouth was still learning how to say: *Monoclonal Gammopathy of Undetermined Significance.* He said the words carefully, as though giving me time to absorb each syllable.

Shock is such a small word for what I felt in that moment. My chest tightened. My hands went clammy. My heart was racing. And then the tears came, and once they started, I couldn't hold them back. It felt like whatever hope I had been holding onto left my body with every single one.

My doctor saw it. He didn't rush me out or hand me a pamphlet and send me on my way. He brought me into his office and sat with me — really sat with me — and let me feel what I was feeling without trying to fix it too quickly. I remember telling him that I was sad. That I was disappointed. That I was scared. But even in that moment, I remember saying to him, '*I don't know if you believe in God or in Jesus — but I do. And He told me not to fear. So that is exactly what I am going to do. I am going to live my life and trust that I will be okay.*'

I don't know where those words came from in that moment. I was still raw. The news was still fresh. But they came — and I meant every one of them.

What made that moment even more profound was who was sitting across from me when I said them. My doctor was from a different culture, one rooted in a different faith entirely. And yet, there I was —heart hurting, hopes deflated, tears barely dry — being used by God to speak the name of Jesus into that room anyway. Not from a pulpit. Not from a place of strength or composure. But from the middle of my own pain.

That is the kind of God He is. He does not wait until we are healed and whole and put together before He sends us out as vessels. He uses us in the very moment of our breaking, when our witness is most raw, most real, and perhaps most powerful. I had prayed for a different outcome that day. I had not gotten it. And yet, somehow, in the middle of that disappointment, God had still found a way to use me for something greater than myself. How profound. How like Him.

I walked out of his office carrying both things at once: the faith I had just declared out loud and the diagnosis I had just been handed. They did not cancel each other out. They simply existed together, the way grief and grace so often do. And as I stepped back out into the ordinary world; the hallway, the parking lot that looked exactly the same as it had an hour ago, the weight of what had just happened began to settle into my bones.

*How do you process hearing that your own blood has turned against you? How do you look at yourself in the mirror the next morning and recognize the person staring back – the person whose story just changed course so sharply?*

*Monoclonal Gammopathy of Undetermined Significance.* Those syllables felt like a foreign language. Like something that belonged in someone else's story, not mine. The doctor said it wasn't cancer. Not now. Not yet. But it was related; a shadow cousin, a possible prelude. What I heard underneath his measured tone was both relief and a warning wrapped into one sentence: "*You're not sick, Brittany, but...*"

In that ellipsis, my mind began to spiral.

He explained that MGUS could stay completely silent for decades. Or it could, quietly and without any fanfare at all, progress into something devastating – Multiple Myeloma.

Multiple Myeloma is a rare and incurable blood cancer. He told me the risk of progression was just one percent per year, as though that statistic was meant to comfort me. But when you are young, when you have dreams still stretching wide open in front of you, one percent does not feel like a small number. One percent feels like a stone you carry in your chest everywhere you go.

It made me think of a patient I had worked with that very same year in the hospital. A man in his seventies, living with the very cancer my body could one day move toward. I remembered him clearly – the way pain had become his constant companion, radiating through his body without mercy. Bones so brittle that the simple act of moving carried the risk of fracture. Anemia so severe it had brought him to the point of blood transfusions just to keep him functional.

I remember thinking, quietly and with everything in me: *this cannot be the life I will live.* Not at his age. Not at any age. I had purpose that had not yet been fulfilled.

I had cared for him with compassion then, the way you do when someone else's suffering is something you can observe but not yet truly inhabit. But sitting in that doctor's office with my own results in hand, I thought of him differently. I thought of him the way you think of someone whose shoes you have just been handed and asked to try on.

Trying on those shoes, I released the version of health I had carried in my young ignorance like a quiet guarantee.... The unspoken contract I believed I had honored: eat reasonably well, move your body, stay away from the things that destroy you, and your body will cooperate in return. That is what we were taught, isn't it?

That office visit cracked that belief wide open.

Health is, at its most honest, an illusion of control; a story we tell ourselves to make the fragility of being human feel more manageable. The truth is far more humbling: we are held completely in the hands of God. Every breath, every heartbeat, every cell dividing quietly within us… all of it beyond our reach. All of it in His.

My ordinary world had been one where nothing was ever seriously wrong. No high blood pressure. No diabetes. No warning signs. I was just Brittany… the one who rarely caught colds in winter and moved through life without ever needing to memorize the names of medications or learn to spell the names of cancers. That version of my life ended in that doctor's office, and I grieved her more than I expected to.

I did what so many of us do when fear takes hold: I imagined the worst. *Would I develop cancer? Would my life end sooner than I ever dreamed? Would the MGUS progress? Would I be okay? Would I see forty? Could I still be a wife? A mother? Would I still be me?*

I catastrophized. Completely and without restraint.

I went home, and I started reading. I devoured medical articles, patient forums, clinical studies, stories of strangers navigating their own diagnoses in the dark corners of the internet. I was trying to make sense of my own story by piecing together pieces of theirs. I learned that MGUS is often discovered by accident, usually with no symptoms – something that simply sits and waits. I read that it appears more frequently in African Americans, that it's rarely present in someone my age, and that people can live - normal, happily, and pain-free - with it for years, even decades. And then I read that *every single case of Multiple Myeloma begins with MGUS.*

That was the part that stayed with me.

I had always thought of myself as strong. Fierce on the basketball court. Resilience in the classroom. Steadfast in my spirit and my faith. I had faced battles before. I had sweated through challenges and prayed my way over obstacles that seemed impossible. But this… This was different. There was no opponent to chase down. No finish line to fix my eyes on. Just a silent, patient, invisible uncertainty living somewhere inside my body, waiting.

At twenty-nine years old, I was facing a diagnosis I did not know how to carry.

It felt almost cruelly ironic that this news arrived just weeks before my thirtieth birthday, a milestone I had genuinely, joyfully looked forward to. Instead of celebrating, I found myself buried under pamphlets filled with terminology I couldn't pronounce, trapped inside a spiral of thoughts about what my life might or might not become. My self-esteem took a blow I had not seen coming. In some quiet and heartbreaking way, I began to feel damaged. Less worthy of love, of dreams, of the beautiful future I had been building.

The hardest part was the waiting rooms.

Every appointment with the hematologist felt like a relentless reminder of my own fragility. I would sit among elderly patients battling their own cancer diagnoses, and the nurses and technicians would look at me and ask, "*Honey, why are you here? You're so young.*" Every time I retold my story, I felt a little more displaced. A little more out of place in my own life.

Beyond those walls, only a few people knew what I was really going through. I had let in only those who I knew could hold the weight of it: my parents, my sister, a few trusted friends, and of course, my husband: by then newlywed and already my steadfast shelter through every storm.

Their reactions reflected everything we were all carrying together: confusion, fear, a helplessness that even the deepest love could not fully dissolve. My father carried a quiet and heavy guilt as though he had somehow passed this pain to me through blood and genetics. My mother, faithful and steady as she has always been, just kept pointing me back to God.

Those who loved me surrounded me with concern, but they were powerless, too. And I understood that.

How often does it happen that when the unimaginable arrives, the people who love us most want desperately to solve what cannot be solved? They search for remedies that might not exist, for words that are never quite enough. But I have learned that sometimes, love can only offer two things: prayer and presence. In that season, I needed both more than I had words to say. And it was my faith, fragile as it was in those early days, that held me together when nothing else could.

I clung to scripture the way you grip a rope in the dark when you cannot see the ground beneath you. Isaiah 41:10 became my daily anchor: "*Fear not, for I am with you; be not dismayed, for I am your God.*" Late at night, I would trace those words softly, speaking them into the quiet of my room, letting each repetition settle a little deeper into the places where fear had taken up residence.

I leaned into worship too. "Jireh" by Elevation Worship became something like medicine for me. There is something about that song that met me exactly where I was: this truth that God would cross an ocean just so I wouldn't drown, that He had never been closer than in the very moment everything felt most uncertain. I didn't need a miracle on a mountaintop. I needed to know that right here, in this fragile and frightening in-between, He was enough. I played it on repeat, letting that truth seep all the way into my bones.

Two years passed before I began to truly understand that my suffering might hold a purpose greater than my own pain.

I didn't wake up one morning suddenly transformed. What I did see — gradually, gently — was a nudge. A redirection. My diagnosis was quietly pulling me back toward the one relationship I had let slip without fully realizing it: my relationship with God.

I remember one particular afternoon, sitting on my mother's couch, carrying fears I couldn't even find the words for. My mother walked in softly and said:

*"Pastor called. He said God told him to tell you… do not fear."*

A Pastor from our old church, someone who had no natural way of knowing what I was wrestling with in silence, had reached out. And the message he carried was the same scripture I had been clinging to in the dark of my room. Isaiah 41:10:

*"Do not fear, for I am with you; do not be dismayed, for I am your God. I will strengthen you and help you; I will uphold you with my righteous right hand."*

I felt something shift deep inside me in that moment. God had seen my silent suffering. And He had responded specifically, personally, unmistakably.

That was the beginning of fear losing its grip on me.

Slowly, I stopped obsessing over prognoses and projections. I started coming back to the present. My prayers changed; they became rawer, more honest. Less polished requests and more genuine wrestling with God. I began to understand that what was happening in my body had a spiritual dimension I could not afford to ignore.

The enemy, I recognized clearly, had intended this health battle to pull me away from God. To use fear and uncertainty to widen the distance between me and the Lord. Maybe even to shorten my days quietly, before my assignment on this earth was ever completed. But it had done the exact opposite. It had driven me straight back into His arms. And the closer I drew, the more I understood that some of what I had been carrying; the dread, the agreements I had made with fear, the cultural scripts about illness and worst-case outcomes, needed to be actively rebuked and renounced in the name of Jesus.

There are things we come into agreement with, sometimes without even realizing it, letting them set up home in the backrooms of our hearts. The words of doctors. The anxious warnings of culture. The tired old scripts of our own doubts. They all want space in your spirit. And I had given them more room than I should have.

In prayer, I began to take that space back. At first it felt like shouting into darkness, as if my words might scatter unheard. But the more I prayed, the more I believed in the power of what God was doing. I wrestled with tear-stained cheeks, then stood back up. I contended for my peace, my healing, my wholeness, not with anger or bitterness, but with an unbending trust in Jehovah El-Roi, the God who sees, and Jehovah Rapha, the God who heals. He was listening. He was already shaping my victory.

My relationship with my own body changed too. I began to understand that this physical frame of mine, with all its imperfections and vulnerabilities, is the temple of the Holy Spirit. God didn't give me just a soul. He housed that soul in this body, this singular vessel, so that I could carry out His purposes right here and right now. Honoring my body became an act of stewardship, attending to my health with care, feeding it well, resting when I needed to, and being genuinely grateful for bones that were still carrying me through seasons of struggle. I stopped punishing myself with harsh inner words. I started listening. I started being thankful.

If you are reading this while carrying a diagnosis that knocked the wind clean out of your dreams, I want to say something directly to you: release what you cannot control. Pour your energy into what you can. For me, that meant anchoring myself in the Word, leaning into faith with both hands, and refusing – absolutely refusing – to come into agreement with fear.

Worry has a way of draining us of the ability to savor the present moment, to find beauty and hope even in the middle of pain. And this life —*your* life – is too sacred to spend it living in a future that hasn't happened yet.

Am I healed? In faith, yes.

Whether the medical reports confirm it today or in the days still ahead, I have chosen my reality: my life belongs to God, and He alone holds my future. What the enemy designed to destroy me, God has turned around for my good. I see that clearly now.

MGUS has a name. But it did not have my story.

It was not the end of my narrative. It was a new chapter, written in ink still wet with hope. I may not know exactly why my body became the battlefield, but I have stopped needing to know. I stopped seeing the diagnosis as punishment and started receiving it as permission: permission to slow down, to strip away everything that wasn't truly serving me, and to anchor myself in faith instead of fear.

And when I think about it now, maybe that is exactly where the real healing begins, not when the blood tests come back normal, but when you stop living like you're dying and start living like you're held...

By God. By grace. By faith.

---

*Refer to the Appendix: Playlist that Held Me for the songs that carried me through this very season. You will find powerful worship that gives breath to hope, even in the ashes.*

# Self-Reflection

1. Have you ever had the experience of feeling "too young" or "too old" for something difficult you were facing? How did that affect you?

2. In what way do you relate to Brittany's feelings of being "damaged" or "defective?" What reassurances can you name that counteract those feelings?

3. Reflect on a time when you prayed but didn't feel immediate answers. What emotions came up?

4. What scriptures, quotes, or songs helped bolster your faith in times of uncertainty?

5. Who have you had in your life that stood there quietly sharing your suffering? Write them a thank-you here.

6. If your body is considered a temple, how are you taking care of it now, physically, spiritually, and emotionally?

7. What part of your healing process still feels unfinished, and what would it look like to surrender that to God?

***Want to go deeper with your reflection?** After you complete this chapter's journal prompts, you can choose to share your answers privately with me. With your consent, your story may be included anonymously in a future devotional sequel.*

# NOTES

..... / .... / ......

S M T W T F S

*What is one thing you don't want to forget from this chapter?*

SPEAK THIS OVER YOURSELF

# My story is not over. Even in the silence, God speaks. Even in the sickness, I still stand. Even in the ashes, I am still whole.

***Father,***

*There are parts of my story I did not see coming. News I was not prepared for. Seasons I would never have chosen. But You were never caught off guard, and You are already present in the middle of it. I bring You the fear that moved in quietly. The worst-case thoughts. The grief of losing the life I thought I was going to have. I release it all. I renounce every agreement I have made with fear and panic. I choose faith over forecast. Your promises over the prognosis. Remind me that my circumstances are not my foundation; You are. That what the enemy intended to break me, You have already determined to use for my good. Where I am still waiting, still afraid, still holding on, please meet me there. You are Jireh. You are enough. And because of You, so am I.*

***In Jesus' name. Amen.***

# III
# ASHES IN MY BLOODLINE

*"We have a high priest who can feel it when*
*we are weak and hurting…"*
*– Heb 4:15 (NIV)*

Why is life so often measured by what we can't control? I've asked myself that question more times than I can count – in the quiet of early mornings, in the chaos of impossible seasons, and in the dark of nights when sleep just wouldn't come. There was a period in my life – one I never would have chosen; one I would never wish on anyone – when health crises didn't just knock at my door. They kicked it clean off the hinges. One after another. My mom. My dad. And somehow, in all of it, me. I want to share it with you because I believe, with everything in me, that there was purpose in every piece of it.

I remember it like it was yesterday. My mother was bustling in the kitchen, her hands certain and sure, the kitchen full of promise and the smell of onions sizzling on the stove. She realized she was missing an ingredient. Of course she did. That's how she was. She was never one to cut corners, never one to let a meal fall short.

She insisted on making a quick dash to the store, not waiting for me. Before I could say a word, I heard the jangle of her keys and the familiar rhythm of her steps heading toward the door. I didn't think twice. I trusted the routine. I trusted the path we had always walked.

Then I heard it. A scream that still lives in the walls of my memory. It wasn't the sharpness of it that broke me. It was the depth. I rushed to the door with my heart already pressing against my ribs before my hands could even turn the knob. And there she was, under the porch light, sprawled across a sheet of black ice, her foot twisted in a way that no foot should ever be. My cousin, a nurse, heard the cries from next door. She came running, already wrapping my mother in a blanket before I could even find my voice.

And me? For all the times I had handled emergencies, for all the years I had trained and prepared and shown up for other people in crisis, in that moment, I was just her daughter. Shaking. Desperate. Dialing 911 with trembling hands and barely steady enough to answer the operator's questions.

Finally, after what must have been fifteen, maybe twenty eternal minutes, they arrived. The paramedics gathered her story; her medical history, her allergies, the small details that define a life, as gently as they could. Then, bundled in blankets and bravery, she was taken away. My dad followed close behind the ambulance.

He was, at first, angry with her for the simplest of reasons. "*Why did you wear those shoes outside?*" he asked, frustration sharpening his voice as he scolded her for stepping out in sneakers that had long lost their grip. No traction left to hold her against the unpredictable ground. Perhaps it's easier to be angry about shoes than to admit that sometimes, life slips out from under us, and there is nothing anyone can do. My parents have known each other their whole lives, and that kind of history is what showed up in this moment. Despite his irritation, my father was there for her. He was ready to help her through recovery.

And so, we followed her there, into the cold, into the unknown, each of us carrying our worry through automatic doors and antiseptic air.

Inside the sterile hospital room, under the buzzing hum of fluorescent lights, my mother's ankle was suddenly at the center of our universe, swollen and broken. The diagnosis was clear: a *trimalleolar fracture* in her right ankle.

A trimalleolar fracture is a fracture involving all three malleoli of the ankle: the lateral malleolus, the medial malleolus, and the posterior malleolus. It is one of the most severe ankle fractures a person can sustain, and seeing it written on that chart beside my mother's name made it terrifyingly real.

Her fracture was so severe they had to reset the bone, cocoon her foot in a temporary cast, and send her home, fragile and hurting, while we awaited the surgery that would anchor her future steps.

I had just quit my job about a week prior; my heart set on moving to Ghana with my husband. My husband and I had already married, exchanging promises of forever across continents. The original plan was simple on paper: I'd join him in Ghana, making our home while he prepared to follow me back to the States. But nothing about life is ever as tidy as an itinerary or a passport stamp.

My flight was two weeks away when my mom fell, and everything I thought I'd prepared for crumbled. I began juggling her business, holding together her finances, praying for guidance, trusting that there would be enough rain for the seeds we had sown.

I became my mother's nurse, her chef, her company-keeper. I tidied counters, made tea, fluffed pillows, and offered the reassurances that I hoped she believed as much as I needed her to: "*You'll be okay. We're getting through this.*" In the middle of it, I saw something I'd never quite noticed before – the silent, stubborn courage that had always lived beneath her daily routine of running a business, being a very active member in her church and caring for her family as she always did.

My mother has always had that singular courage of growing her business from the heart and hands of our home. When she was hurt, everything paused. Except me. I stepped quietly into her shoes, and I knew exactly how they fit. I had worked alongside her since high school, through undergrad, learning the rhythms of what she had built long before I fully understood what it had cost her to build it. So, when she couldn't stand, I stood in her place. Between running her business, preparing meals, managing paperwork, and packing for my impending move to Ghana, I sometimes forgot to breathe. I was doing so much. More than I ever said out loud.

And yet, even in the middle of all of it, gratitude found me. Its timing felt less like *coincidence* and more like *intention*. No one could have planned for this. But looking back, I can see clearly what I couldn't see then: had I still been busy with the chaos of working in the hospital, there would have been no margin to help my family the way they needed. What once felt like a risky, even uncertain move quietly revealed itself to be divine provision. The Lord had placed me exactly where I needed to be, before I even knew I would need to be there.

As I walked that road of recovery with my mother, I realized I, too, was cracked and aching in unseen places, wounds pressed deep into the soft tissue of my spirit. For a year or more, every sudden noise, every strange cry or crash in the distance, echoed with the terror of those cold hours. My heart would gallop. My nervous system transformed into a jittery guard, always braced for the next catastrophe. My mind was hyper-vigilant, tuning into any sign that something else, anything new, could go wrong. I'd have to remind myself, aloud sometimes, that the world wasn't falling apart… not again, not this time.

That hypervigilance kept my nervous system scanning for threats, every moment loaded with the possibility of more bad news. And yet, amid the constant threat detection, there was one thing we could anchor to: her surgery had been scheduled for six days after the diagnosis. That appointment became our fragile lifeline, a tiny structure in the chaos of waiting.

That same weekend my mother was bracing for her ankle surgery, my father (a man who had always seemed immune to weakness) grew quiet about a persistent ache in his side. He didn't tell me. Only later did I learn he'd asked a friend to drive him to urgent care, because he thought it was nothing, maybe something small. But the clinic's doctor pressed a hand to his side, felt something lurking there, and sent him on to the emergency room with an expression that said this was anything but small.

My father ended up in a different hospital across town. And I found myself weaving between two fears, two buildings, two people I loved. Each in a different kind of pain.

It was close to 1 a.m. – that same night – when my phone rang. The voice on the other end delivered news no one ever feels ready to hear: my father had been diagnosed with stage three colon cancer. I felt my body go completely still.

And then, I wept.

I wept for my father, alone in a hospital room with news I am certain he wasn't prepared for. I wept for my mother, enduring surgery on the other side of town. I wept for both of them, and honestly, I wept for myself. My phone, now heavy and useless in my hand, sat on my lap as I tried to make sense of a world so suddenly rearranged.

Only a week before, both my parents were perfectly fine. And now, in less than a fortnight, they had each been swallowed by hospital corridors in ways I could not fix with tender words. *How could comfort turn into loneliness so swiftly? The tears…* My tears poured out so fast and so heavy.

The house I knew from childhood felt empty and echoing. For the first time, the absence of my parents (still alive, but away) gave me a terrifying glimpse of what true loss might be. The house felt strange, as if it too were in mourning, holding its breath in solidarity with the heaviness that now haunted its rooms. I imagined outcomes I could barely voice; *would my mom make it through recovery? Would my dad come home again?*

Every headline I'd ever read about cancer whispered at me in the dark. Stage three. The words felt like a death sentence, heavy and final. Was my dad about to die? Was this the chapter I wasn't ready to close?

Through the storm of my thoughts, another truth came into focus, my mother's calm acceptance. Later, she would share that my dad had been keeping quiet about his pain, brushing it off in the way only stubborn men can. She told him to see a doctor, but he tucked himself into denial. That struck me - how often we try to protect the people we love by pretending we're fine, how much we hide under the guise of strength.

From the deepest part of myself, I used to look up and ask, "Why?" Why was health all of a sudden center stage in my life? Why were people I loved being swept up into illness and suffering—one after another, as if pain was stalking my footprints? Like anyone who's tried to make sense of unexpected circumstances, my thoughts occasionally spiraled into doubt. *Was it me? Was there something connected to my existence that made the people closest to me more vulnerable to attack? Had I done something so wrong, so unforgivable, that my loved ones were suffering because of my mistakes?*

I knew, deep down, that I hadn't committed any earth-shattering wrongs, that God, angry and vengeful, would strike me down by punishing the people I loved and hold so dearly. Still, I couldn't help but wonder.

When bad things stack up one after another and you're desperate to make sense of the senseless, your mind can invent patterns where none exist. That's what we call, as professionals in my field, trauma/cognitive processing or cognitive distortions. We crave answers so fiercely that, when the world gives us randomness, our minds try to string together our own explanations from the sometimes disconnected dots.

There's a scripture I cling to, reminding me that God's ways are not ours, His thoughts not our thoughts. Things happen, sometimes cruelly, and we don't always get our "why." I reached out to spiritual leaders during those foggy days, and they listened patiently to my fears. They gently reminded me: *Brittany, this is not your fault.* I wanted desperately to believe them, but belief doesn't always arrive on command; it creeps in slow especially when grief clouds your sight.

It didn't always make the pain smaller, but it kept me from drowning in the questions.

The day of my mom's surgery arrived, carrying with it a mix of dread and desperate hope. They worked carefully to repair what had been so violently undone, keeping her in the hospital for three long days where every update felt like holding my breath. Finally, they sent her home, fragile but fighting.

The surgery was only the beginning. For weeks afterward, she moved through physical therapy with fierce determination, learning again how to bear weight on that tender ankle, how to trust the ground beneath her when every step whispered doubt, how to make peace with pain that would not disappear overnight.

And even while she was still recovering, still faithfully showing up to therapy through the ache and exhaustion, my father was still in the hospital too.

My father's situation carried its own weight. His insurance was limited, his disability benefits nowhere near enough. The needs multiplied with every day he spent in that hospital room, and we had to get creative. Thankfully, my father's name carried something that money couldn't manufacture; a reputation built over decades of showing up for his community. He had poured himself into coaching young people, giving his weekends, his evenings, his laughter and his discipline to children who needed someone to believe in them. He had sown generously into other people's lives for years. And now, it was time to believe that same community would return what he had given.

We set up a fundraiser. And just like that, our private pain stepped outside the walls of our house and became part of a larger story, one that invited the generosity and compassion of people who had been waiting for a chance to give back. I was not prepared for what happened next.

Donations came in envelopes and phone calls and prayers spoken over us from people we hadn't spoken to in years. I will never forget the flood of it; the sheer, overwhelming warmth of being loved by a community that showed up without being asked twice. It reminded me that there is just as much grace in learning to receive as there has ever been in giving.

That fundraiser gave us the strength to keep climbing. And we would need every bit of it because my father's journey with cancer was not a sprint. It wasn't even a marathon. It was a continual, relentless climb with no clear summit in sight. I remember the first time he came out of surgery. He looked like a man trying to find himself inside a body that had become unfamiliar, searching for the version of himself he recognized, in a face and a frame that the disease through the surgery had quietly rearranged.

My father is not a man who says much about what he feels. Pain finds its own language in quiet men, and I saw traces of something in him, maybe resentment for the years he had brushed aside routine doctor appointments, believing himself unbreakable until his own body proved him wrong. Still, in the only way he knew how, he squared his jaw, looked everyone in the eye, and said: *I'm just going to do what I can do to beat it and see what happens.*

Those weren't dramatic words. They weren't battle cries. They were just a man finding his footing in the ashes.

What followed was a long, grinding climb. Three surgeries. Radiation. Rounds of treatment that chiseled away at the body he had always relied on. The first surgery was a major change. They took most of his small intestine in hopes of removing most if not all of the cancer. An ostomy bag became his new reality. For months, his most private bodily functions were carried outside of him in a plastic pouch, and I watched a strong man navigate the humbling, daily reality of a body that no longer worked the way it used to.

Then another shadow was found. Another stretch of him claimed by disease. Another surgery followed, and with it, another version of life he had to learn to inhabit.

The body he woke up to after that was not the one he had always known. It demanded new rhythms, new boundaries, new negotiations. The way he ate changed. The pace at which he moved through his days changed. Rest, once something he had to be convinced to take, became not a luxury but a requirement. He was learning, slowly and without a manual, how to live inside a body that had been rearranged by survival; a body that was his, and yet unfamiliar. Temporary in its current form, he hoped. But present, and demanding to be honored, in the meantime.

After several months, words that we hoped would come sooner than later: *We're going to reverse the ostomy.*

The third and final surgery. The bag was removed. Piece by careful piece, they knit him whole again.

And the news came.

**Cancer-free!**

My father walked outside into the light, whole.

He came home from the hospital a calmer man, and somehow, a wiser one. He spoke earnestly now of changing his ways. He had begun to see the body as a trust from God; something to be cared for, not pushed to its limits with greasy meals, sugary snacks, and just one more fried indulgence. Fresh vegetables took the place of potato chips. Grilled fish replaced fried pork. Regular doctor visits became a pillar, not a punishment. And daily walks became his norm.

The lesson reverberated through our whole family: you cannot simply hope or pray that struggle will pass you by while you ignore the very things that cultivate it. Your body is God's temple — fleeting and precious — and it deserves reverence.

I want to be clear-eyed with you about what I know and what I don't know. In America, colon cancer accounts for the vast majority of colorectal cancer deaths — over 957,000 lives lost in just a two-decade span, an average of more than 130 people every single day.[1]

---

[1] *Beaumont Health / Corewell Health Research. "Changes in US Colorectal Cancer Mortality Trends Over the Past 20 Years." Scholarly Works, January 2024.*

Those aren't numbers. Those are mothers, fathers, daughters, sons, friends. Every one of them a story that never got its final chapter.

I couldn't help but think of Chadwick Boseman, the king in *Black Panther*, the symbol of strength for so many who had never seen themselves crowned on screen. Lost at just 43. The same disease. A very different ending. His loss shook me to my bones. Because survival, I've come to understand, is not merit. It is grace.

Before I move forward, I want to pause here — because if you have walked through anything like what I've just described, there are three things I need you to know.

The first is this: what your body is doing makes sense.

Even when the surgeries were behind us and the words "*cancer-free*" finally filled the room like something sacred, I noticed that something inside of me was still braced. Still waiting. Still scanning. My heart would race at sounds that meant nothing. My shoulders carried tension I hadn't consciously chosen. Sleep came shallow, if it came at all. Even in the quiet moments, the ones that should have felt like relief, some part of me was still on guard, still listening for the next thing to go wrong.

That is what compounding trauma does. When crisis doesn't wait for the last one to finish before the next one arrives, it doesn't only disrupt your circumstances. It gets into your body. Into the very way you move through a room, answer a phone, or hear a sudden noise in the middle of the night. The brain adapts to protect you. It learns to brace for impact before impact arrives. And for a season, that is a gift. But when the danger has passed and your body still hasn't gotten the message, that protection quietly becomes exhaustion.

Some might call that exhaustion weakness. And maybe, on the surface, it can look that way. But I want you to know you are not disqualified from God's care because of it. In fact, it is precisely there, in that place of weariness and frayed nerves, that He is most near. Scripture reminds us that we have a high priest who can feel it when we are weak and hurting; we have One who, in every respect, has been tested as we are. He is not standing at a distance, unmoved by your trauma. He sees it. He knows it. He has felt the weight of a body under pressure.

So cast it. Every anxious thought, every tight shoulder, every sleepless night. Cast it on Him, because He cares for you. Not in spite of what you are feeling, but because of it. Trauma is not a sign that your faith has failed. It is an invitation to experience a God who does not just heal the soul in theory, but who meets you in the very body that is struggling to find its way back to rest.

The second thing I want you to know is this: trauma doesn't always look the way you expect it to.

Sometimes it looks like irritability, or the need to control everything around you. Sometimes it looks like numbness, a flatness you can't quite explain. And sometimes, if you're anything like me, it looks like over-functioning. Doing everything for everyone, holding every single piece together, because some part of you believes that if you just stay busy enough, nothing else will fall apart.

I want you to release the guilt that whispers, *Why am I not over this yet?* You see, you are not broken. Your body was protecting you. It simply needs, now, to be gently retrained toward safety.

And the third thing (the one I most want you to carry with you) is that the brain that learned survival can also learn peace.

It is not a mystical process. It begins in small, unglamorous moments. Breathing deeply enough to signal to your own body: *I am safe right now.* Placing your feet flat on the floor and letting your eyes take in the room around you. Naming what you feel instead of pushing it back down. Letting people help you without the weight of shame. Replacing the spiral of catastrophic thinking with something grounded and true: *Right now, in this moment, nothing is happening.* Over time, those small moments of safety become new pathways. The body softens. The hypervigilance loosens its grip, little by little.

I've come to believe that God does not only heal through miracles in operating rooms, though He absolutely can, and in my father's case, He did. He also heals through breath. Through community. Through rest. Through the quiet, unglamorous work of rewiring. Through teaching our bodies what our faith is already trying to tell us: *We survived. We are still here. And peace is possible.*

Healing is not just spiritual. It is neurological. Not just emotional. It is biological. And like everything else the Lord has walked me through, it happens in the surrendering, not the striving.

# Self-Reflection

1. Where in my life do I still feel "on guard," even though the danger has passed? What might my body be trying to protect me from?

______________________________________________

______________________________________________

______________________________________________

______________________________________________

2. What physical sensations do I notice in my body when I feel anxious or overwhelmed, and what might those sensations be trying to communicate?

______________________________________________

______________________________________________

______________________________________________

______________________________________________

3. Have I ever mistaken exhaustion for weakness? What if my exhaustion is actually evidence of what I've survived?

______________________________________________

______________________________________________

______________________________________________

______________________________________________

4. What truths can I hold onto when my mind begins to spiral into fear or worst-case scenarios?

______________________________________________

______________________________________________

______________________________________________

______________________________________________

5. What guilt am I carrying for not "healing fast enough"? Who told me I needed to rush my healing?

______________________________________________

______________________________________________

______________________________________________

______________________________________________

6. What small, grounding practices can I begin to introduce into my daily life to remind my body that I am safe?

______________________________________________

______________________________________________

______________________________________________

______________________________________________

7. How has trauma shaped the way I think, react, or relate to others, and what parts of that am I ready to gently unlearn?

______________________________________________

______________________________________________

______________________________________________

______________________________________________

***Want to go deeper with your reflection?*** *After you complete this chapter's journal prompts, you can choose to share your answers privately with me. With your consent, your story may be included anonymously in a future devotional sequel.*

# NOTES

..... / .... / ......

S M T W T F S

*Sit here a little longer...*
*What else is God saying to you?*

SPEAK THIS OVER YOURSELF

# I am not alone. God is with me. Guiding me. Sustaining me. Surrounding me. With His Unending love.

***Heavenly Father,***
*I come to You tired; tired in my body, my mind, and the places in between that I don't always have words for. You see every hard moment I am carrying. You see the fears I haven't spoken out loud, the weight I have been holding in silence. And even in all of it, You are faithful. Where my body is still braced for impact, still scanning for the next thing to go wrong, meet me there. When life stacks crisis upon crisis, and I cannot find the bottom of it, remind me that You are still writing. Help me to stop striving and start surrendering. And when I cannot see the end of my story, help me to trust You the Author.*
***In Jesus' name, Amen.***

# IV
# ASHES IN MY BLOODLINE, STILL

*"Now tell them this:*
*'As surely as I live, declares the LORD,*
*I will do to you the very things I heard you say."*
*– Numbers 14:28 (NLT)*

The house felt too quiet that afternoon, heavy with the weight of everything unsaid. I found my mother resting on the couch, her bandaged ankle propped up, her face etched with the kind of exhaustion that comes from fighting invisible battles. My heart pounded as I sank beside her, the words I'd been carrying like stones finally tumbling out.

"*Mom,*" I whispered, my voice cracking, "*should I even go? To Ghana? With everything happening, is this the sign I should stay? That my dreams need to wait?*"

She turned to me then, her eyes beaming with a mother's unyielding love. "*Brittany,*" she said softly but with steel beneath it, "*you were made to chase what God put in your heart. Go. Live your life. Whatever is happening here, we will figure it out.*"

Those words anchored me through the whirlwind days that followed. My sister arrived from Texas like an answer to prayer, stepping seamlessly into the caregiving role I'd held: cooking, appointments, the endless small acts of love, so I could keep my promise to my husband.

And so, with my parents blessing wrapped around me like a shield, I boarded the plane for Ghana. I carried my hopes for a new chapter across the ocean, even as the grief of leaving them behind clung tight.

For over a year, I tried to settle into that new chapter. I exhaled, slowly and carefully, the way you do when you're afraid that breathing too deeply might invite the next storm. And for a while, the quiet held.

Then, in the summer of 2022, my phone rang from home.

My mother had been rushed to the hospital.

Doctors confirmed her appendix had become inflamed to the point of near rupture: acute appendicitis. I understood exactly what it meant. If they hadn't caught it in time, if she had waited even a day longer, dismissed the pain the way we so often dismiss the things quietly threatening to undo us, the outcome could have been unthinkable. Acute appendicitis does not announce itself politely. It strikes silently, swiftly, and without warning.

So, I did what anxious people do. I Googled. And what I found both terrified and steadied me: more than 300,000 people in the United States alone face this same emergency every year.[2]

---

[2] *Hatch, Quinton. "Appendicitis." In StatPearls. Treasure Island, FL: StatPearls Publishing, 2024. National Institutes of Health, National Library of Medicine.*

It was more common than I'd imagined. And yet, sitting alone with my phone thousands of miles away, it felt like it was only happening to us.

The procedure they performed was a laparoscopic appendectomy; a surgery that, for all its clinical precision, carries a kind of quiet miracle in it. Rather than opening the body wide, surgeons make only the smallest of incisions, guided by a tiny camera threaded inside, navigating the body's hidden landscape to remove the threat before it becomes catastrophe. It is medicine at its most careful and deliberate. And in my mother's case, that careful, precise intervention was the difference between a close call and something I am not ready to write about.

I was thousands of miles away, and there was nothing I could do but pray and wait.

It felt as though something had made it its mission to test us. To choreograph emergency after emergency, to send wave after wave crashing against our shores just as we were finally learning to breathe between them. Every time I thought we had steadied ourselves, every time I dared believe that the worst was behind us, another door would swing open and demand our courage all over again.

But God.

Those two words are a complete sentence in my family. They always have been. *But God,* He held her through it. The surgery was successful. My mother came through. And once again, what could have been a tragedy became a testimony.

Yet, as I would discover again and again, life never consults us before it changes everything.

Barely a month later, my phone rang again.

It was my sister calling, and the moment I picked up, I knew. There are certain silences on a phone line that speak before any words do — a held breath, a hesitation — and in that split second, my heart was already bracing. Then I heard it. Not my sister's voice. My mother's. A scream. Raw and wrenching. It cut through the miles between us and landed somewhere deep in the pit of my soul.

"*What's happening?*" I kept asking, my own voice unraveling. "*What's going on?*"

My sister's voice was shaky. "*We don't know. Mommy's saying her stomach hurts.*"

A wave of panic swept over me. My cousin, the same nurse who had rushed to our side during the ankle incident, rushed again to my mother. In those moments, our family's network of love snapped into action. Calls were made. And soon, an ambulance was pulling up to my mother's door.

She was back in the hospital.

This time, doctors discovered a *rectus abdominis muscle hematoma*. A blood clot that had formed, cold and stubborn, at the very site where her appendix had been removed.

A rectus abdominis muscle hematoma is exactly as serious as it sounds. It occurs when blood collects inside the sheath surrounding the abdominal muscles (often triggered by surgery, trauma, or the body's own fragile response to healing) pooling where it should not, pressing against tissue, refusing to disperse on its own. It is painful, unpredictable, and in severe cases, can become life-threatening. It is the kind of complication that reminds you that healing is rarely ever a straight line.

And my mother was living proof of that. Even now, I remember the particular weight of that worry – how it settled in my chest differently from the others, because this time it felt not just frightening, but deeply unfair. My mother, who had already endured so much, who had already surrendered so much of herself to hospital beds and recovery rooms and the slow, grinding work of healing, was now handed yet another reason to fight.

But she did not have to face another scalpel. This time, mercifully, the treatment was medication and time. And through all of it, her spirit never dimmed.

From afar, I felt pulled home by the force of our connection. I was helpless to change her pain, but present in every other way I could be – FaceTiming and praying and praying and FaceTiming. My sister became my lifeline, updating me with texts throughout Mom's hospital days. Being physically separated from the ones you love adds a new layer of helplessness that no one tells you about, a kind of ache that lives in the space between a video call and a real embrace. Yet God, in His mercy, gave me companionship. My husband was near; gentle in his presence, holding space for my grief, offering comfort even when I didn't have language for my pain. Above all else, the most steadfast companion was my faith.

It might sound cliché, unless you've lived a moment where only faith gives you footing. I truly put it all in God's hands. I remembered all those surgeries my mother had already survived. Her ankle. Her appendix. And I prayed: *Father, You got her through then, I trust You'll get her through now.* I repeated that to myself so often it became a lullaby for my soul. I made an active choice, every morning, to hope instead of drown. I spoke life over the situation, not death. When fear knocked, I met it with a stubborn, deliberate positivity. I guarded my thoughts – tended them like fragile new shoots, aligning my mind with Proverbs 4:23: "*Guard your heart above all else, for it determines the course of your life.*" Left unchecked, negativity will run wild and sap the life right out of hope.

Some days I'd find myself thinking long and hard, I wondered when, or even *if*, the storm would ever still.

Underneath it all, I prayed. I prayed more in those nights than I remember praying in my entire life. For mercy. For resilience. For some measure of peace. And most of all, for healing.

I didn't want my parents to die. That's the raw truth. In the deep places of my heart, I didn't. In those darkened days, when questions shook the very essence of my soul, I pleaded with God; not for grand answers, but simply for *time*. For more birthdays. More laughter ringing through the house. More Sunday afternoons where their voices drifted in and out of rooms, as familiar as the smell of bread warming in the oven.

My parents were both in their fifties; still moving through life with purpose and plans. Losing them was a possibility, yes. But a later one. A faraway one. At least, that's what I told myself.

But one day you wake up and realize that death isn't polite enough to knock. It doesn't wait for children to grow up all the way, for relationships to mend, for forgiveness to be spoken aloud. I found myself waiting, worrying, begging, praying. My plea was always the same, always simple: *Father, please don't let them go. Not now. Not yet. I'm not ready.*

These prayers became my morning and midnight ritual. I had to learn to pray with a heart that believed in the possibility of healing, and also in the certainty of God's presence through every uncertain turn.

And then they were both healed.

Completely. Wholly. Not partially restored, not managing their conditions from a distance, but genuinely, miraculously, undeniably free.

When healing finally came for both of them, I felt like I was watching the divine up close. Twice, I had stood at the threshold where fear meets faith, and every single time, Jehovah Rapha reached across the divide and stitched my parents' wounds with unseen hands. It changed me. It made me braver. Their healing taught me that rising from ashes can become a family legacy, when God is in the story.

I learned quickly how fragile everything was. The plans we make, the small routines that feel so permanent, the people we assume will always be there… none of it was promised. My awareness sharpened. I started noticing things I had taken for granted. I said *I love you* more. I offered gratitude more freely. I forgave more, and faster, loosening my grip on grudges and old disappointments that suddenly felt too small and too heavy to carry at the same time. I let people know, again and again, just how much they meant to me. And more than anything, I chose to show up present for the people I loved, because presence, I had learned, is the most sacred gift we can offer one another.

When people ask me how I kept showing up every day; the truth is, I don't think I did it consciously. It happened the way a river knows which way is down. The way a flower leans toward the sun without deciding to. There is a strength inside us that hides in reserve, only revealing itself when life presses us hard enough to need it.

In that season, my singular focus was caring for my parents. That focus became the anchor. It was love, pure and simple, pulling me forward when my own legs threatened to give out. I found myself lifted, carried along as if held in hands I couldn't see.

Indeed, I was held.

Life became less about waiting for tomorrow and more about embracing today, being *present,* really present, with the people I loved. I began to understand how thin the veil is between what we think we have and what can be taken in an instant. And in that understanding, a deep gratitude took root. Gratitude for breath, for laughter, for family, for love. Gratitude for *now.*

If you are walking this road, if your parents or loved ones are facing illness, I want you to know you are not alone. When you feel the sting of doubt and the weight of vulnerability, speak healing over your life and the lives of those you love. Let your prayers be declarations; firm and full of faith that God heals by the stripes of His only begotten Son, Jesus the Christ. Say it out loud: *I believe in healing. I believe that restoration is possible.* Stand in that belief, even when the evidence seems thin, even when despair lingers at the edges.

Guard your hope. Let it be your compass on the bleakest days. There are too many voices that will tell you what is impossible, what is lost. But hope is the truest thing I can offer you, from one survivor to another, from the ashes I have known and risen from. Hold it close. Let it guide you home, again and again.

Then, I must remind you of David and Goliath because that story never gets old when you're in the middle of a battle that feels too big for your hands.

Long before David ever faced Goliath, he spent his days in the fields, his only company the sheep, and the lion and the bear that would threaten them. God used David's time in the wilderness to teach him how to fight. Those smaller battles were his dry runs. His training ground. So, when the giant stood before him, David could look King Saul in the eye and say with absolute certainty: "*Your servant has killed both lion and bear; and this uncircumcised Philistine will be like one of them... seeing he has defied the armies of the living God*" (1 Samuel 17:36).

There is such power in that declaration. It is not denial of the threat. It is not naive boasting. It is a statement *forged in the heat of earlier battles*; a proclamation that because God has shown up before, He will not abandon you now. Anything that dares to defy what God has promised over you cannot have the last word. Even when the threat towers above you, it too will bow — in time.

The real test came when the phone calls arrived, one after another, carrying words like *acute appendicitis, hematoma, cancer.* Each word a Goliath. Taunting and towering. They didn't just threaten the people who raised me; they felt like defiance against the healing power of the God who created me. They stood in the center of my world and declared war.

But like David, God in His infinite wisdom had walked me through smaller battles first; lending me victories so that when these giants stood before me, I would know exactly what to do. I looked at them, named them for what they were: imposters defying the armies of the living God. That is how I chose to see cancer, acute appendicitis, hematoma. Goliaths, standing defiantly against the God of Abraham, Isaac, Jacob – and my family.

They had to go.

My own health battles had been my lions and my bears. When my parents' diagnoses came, I already had *history* with God. That history became my slingshot. Faith became my backbone; a steady voice in the dark that says: *Remember. Every lion, and every bear was meant to prepare you for the Goliaths yet to come.*

When, by God's mercy, the Goliaths were finally out of the way, when I was climbing out from the valley of my parents' diagnoses, my prayers were intense. Sometimes desperate. I begged. I pleaded.

"*Dear Lord,*" I'd pray. "*Please… please let this be the last battle. Please let me know peace. Please, Lord.*"

I clung to hope that maybe – just maybe – my chapter in the Book of Hard Times was drawing to a close.

But life…

Life, in its endless syllabus of lessons, revealed otherwise.

# Self-Reflection

1. In what ways have you experienced repeated challenges that made you wonder, "When will this end?" How did you keep going?

2. Looking back, can you identify a moment where God was quietly working behind the scenes, even when everything felt out of control?

3. What is one declaration of faith you can begin to speak daily over your life and your loved ones, regardless of your current circumstances?

4. In what ways have past "lion and bear" battles prepared you for current "Goliath" situations?

5. When both her parents were healed, Brittany saw the faithfulness of God in her bloodline. Write down one way God's faithfulness has shown up in your family.

6. This chapter reminds us of the fragile gift of time with loved ones. Who is one person you feel God is asking you to cherish more intentionally?

7. Fear of loss can be paralyzing, but Brittany learned to release her fear in prayer. What are you most afraid of losing right now? Have you honestly brought that fear before God?

***Want to go deeper with your reflection?*** *After you complete this chapter's journal prompts, you can choose to share your answers privately with me. With your consent, your story may be included anonymously in a future devotional sequel.*

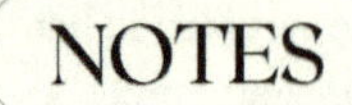

..... / .... / ......

S M T W T F S

*What did this chapter unlock in you that you still need to pour out?*

SPEAK THIS OVER YOURSELF

# Fear has no hold on me. Faith is my shield. Grace is my covering. Restoration is my portion.

**Dear Lord,**

*I come before You carrying the weight of watching the people I love suffer, and the helplessness of not being able to fix it. Meet me in that place. Remind me that You are Jehovah Rapha, the God who heals, and that no diagnosis, no distance, and no darkness is too deep for Your hand to reach. When the giants in my life stand tall and taunting, remind me of every lion and every bear You have already walked me through. Let my history with You become my confidence. Let the battles I have survived become the slingshot I carry into the ones still ahead. Guard my heart. When fear threatens to swallow my hope whole, help me to speak life over myself and the ones I love.* ***In Jesus' name, Amen.***

# V
# ASHES OF AN EMPTY CRADLE

*"Even if the fig tree does not bloom and the vines have no grapes,*
*even if the olive tree fails to produce and the fields yield no food,*
*even if the sheep pen is empty and the stalls have no cattle –*
*even then, I will be happy with the Lord.*
*I will truly find joy in God, who saves me."*
*– Habakkuk 3:17-18 (GW)*

For as long as I can remember, I have carried the image of a baby in my arms. Not as a passing fantasy, but as something woven into the fabric of who I am. The smell of powder and warm milk. The weight of a tiny body curled against my chest. The sound of a lullaby humming itself through a room softened by night. That picture lived inside me long before I had words for it, long before my body understood what it would ask of me to carry it into reality.

I came into that longing early. Being eleven years old and becoming an aunt has a way of doing that to you. I didn't just observe from a distance; I stepped in. I helped. I held and rocked and soothed. Nurturing came to me the way breathing does: naturally, without having to think about it. My nieces and nephews were never just family to me. They were practice. They were proof. They were an early glimpse of what I already knew, deep in my bones, I was made for.

On December 12th, 2020, beneath Ghana's wide, warm skies, my heart found its rhythm. I became a bride. There is something I will never forget about that day; not just its beauty, but the sense of divine alignment I felt, as though God had spent years quietly arranging a moment He always knew was coming. His friends told him he was lucky. They said it again and again, like luck was the only language they had for what they were witnessing. And maybe they were right in more ways than they realized, because I felt the blessing too. I felt it in my chest like a second heartbeat. *We had both been chosen.*

With marriage came the natural unfolding of something I had waited for my whole life: the real and burning possibility of children. It ignited almost immediately, as instinctive as breath, as necessary as water. We were married. We were in love. We were ready. I honestly believed that was all life required. I had no idea, yet, how much more patience it would ask of me.

Reality, I would learn, does not read from the same page as hope.

Month after month, the calendar kept turning. Twelve full cycles of wanting. Twelve cycles of building something beautiful in my mind, only to face the quiet devastation of arms still empty. By most medical standards, six months of trying is not even considered cause for concern. Doctors will say that with a steady, practiced calm that nearly breaks you: *give it time, give it time, give it time.* But time in matters of the heart does not obey statistics or charts. Each month compressed itself into an eternity. Every negative test felt like a whispered *no* delivered directly to my spirit. An invisible barrier between me and the very thing I had prayed for.

People I loved (people close to me who had struggled, just as we had), began to conceive. To welcome life. And there I was, doing everything I believed to be "right," holding my breath month after month, watching what I was praying for land softly in the laps of others. I am not ashamed to tell you that my initial reaction was a tangled braid of feelings I could not neatly separate. Genuine happiness for people I loved. And underneath it – quiet, sharp, unspoken – a sorrow that was entirely my own. I cheered for them out loud. And I grieved privately. I don't think I was wrong to do either.

Social media, during that season, became something I had to be careful with.

Every scroll brought me face-to-face with baby bumps and baby shower reels, with balloon arches and glowing mothers, with swaddled newborns cradled by beaming friends. Images that, on any other day, would have simply made me smile. But in that season? They pricked at something raw. There were moments when I felt my breath catch mid-scroll, my chest squeeze tight, and I knew – not out of bitterness, but out of self-preservation – that I needed to step away. I muted notifications. I curated carefully what I let in.

This wasn't avoidance. I want to be clear about that. It was healthy coping. As a therapist, I know the difference. I didn't have control over what my body was or wasn't doing. I didn't have control over God's timing. But I could identify what I needed in order to persevere, and I could choose to protect my tenderness. True friendship, true love, and true joy for others don't require that you sacrifice your own healing to prove them.

I wish I could tell you I held steady and unshaken through all of it. That my faith never flickered. But the real story is messier than that, and I made a promise to be honest here.

*Why not me? Why not us?*

The questions started quietly. Then they became relentless. They tapped on the walls of my mind at odd hours.

*Is something wrong with me? Are we not worthy of this? Have I disappointed God? Am I being punished? Did I do something wrong? Did I fail to do something right? What is it about us that disqualifies us from this gift?*

There is a specific kind of sorrow that lives inside hope delayed. A heaviness that tints everything: the way you think, the way you feel, the way you read a room or scroll your phone or sit in church. I felt it. Some nights, my heart felt genuinely empty, and resentment pressed in like an unwelcome houseguest threatening to crowd out everything I still loved about God. I wanted to cry out, *Why are You silent now?* I wanted to know if my prayers were actually landing anywhere, or just floating up into the air and falling back down, voiceless and unheard.

Yet – and this is important – even in my anger, I did not leave.

There is a verse in Habakkuk that I kept returning to during that season, almost against my will. The prophet essentially says – *even if nothing blooms, even if the vines are bare, even if the fields produce nothing, even if the pens are empty and the stalls are silent* — even then, I will find joy in God. Even then. Not because the circumstances changed. Not because the answer finally came. But because He was still God in the emptiness of it all.

That scripture felt less like comfort and more like a challenge at first. A dare, almost. *Can you praise Me here? In the bare fields? In the empty pen? In the month that ended with nothing again?* And slowly — not all at once, but slowly — I found that I could. Not perfectly. Not without tears. But I could.

My fury did not exile me from faith. It lived alongside it. And somehow, in that tension between my anger and my worship, God met me anyway.

My doctor kept telling me the same thing, visit after visit. *Everything looks good. Give it time. Don't stress. Let it happen.* Platitudes that sounded like paper-thin promises after a while; always floating just out of reach. But the one voice that never sounded hollow to me was my husband's.

He found me in those dark moments. Every time. He would gather me up with his words, steady and warm, and remind me that faith is not reserved for the good days.

*"Hold on, love. The right time is coming. God hasn't forgotten us."*

Sometimes that was comforting. I'll be honest, sometimes it was annoying. To be that broken and have someone beside you who could still see the sunrise when you were stumbling through the night. But I was grateful for it. He was my anchorage. Every time I drifted too far into despair, he brought me back.

I asked him, lovingly and persistently, to consider getting checked. It seemed practical. If we were in this together, shouldn't we face every possibility together? He smiled in that way I couldn't quite read; not resistant, exactly, but settled in his faith. He had his reservations about Ghana's medical system, and I honored that. Instead, he sought counsel quietly, through a trusted friend who was a doctor, and he would come home and share what he'd learned. We'd sit with those words together, weighing them against our fears and our hopes. I understand now, through my own training as a therapist, that infertility and loss can have roots on both sides — that male genetic factors and sperm health are too often overlooked, leaving women to carry a disproportionate weight of guilt and self-questioning. Knowing that didn't just inform my clinical work. It quietly freed something in me.

By months six, seven, eight... I felt something inside me reckon with a question I didn't want to ask out loud: *What more can I do, God?*

So, we did what we could. We changed our diets. We researched. We tried supplements. We started morning walks. We became students of wellness blogs and fertility forums and every theory we could find, doing all within our human power to signal to God that we were ready. And then we did something that I think saved us.

We started naming the children we couldn't see yet.

Late nights, sitting together, speaking wishes out loud into the empty air of rooms our children hadn't yet filled. *If it's a girl...* We agreed on Elisa: God's promise, God is a promise. Nyameama: gift of God, from the Akan tradition. Sarfo. Names we held like seeds, turning them over carefully in our hands. We couldn't agree on a boy's name. But speaking their names out loud was its own kind of prayer. It was a rebellion against defeat. It was us daring to call what we could not yet see into the light of language, insisting on the possibility of their existence before the evidence arrived.

Those conversations made me feel like our children were already nearby. Just waiting at the edges of our lives to be called home.

There were days I questioned this body I'd been given to live in.

*Is this happening because of my diagnosis? Is my body betraying me? What if it can't do the very thing everyone said it would?*

Society screams at women that we are built for this. That motherhood waits for us like a birthright. So, what do you do when your body sends you a different signal? I questioned my value. I asked myself things I am almost embarrassed to write down, but I'll write them anyway because someone reading this needs to know she is not alone for having thought them. *Would I still count? If I couldn't give life, what was my purpose here?*

I didn't handle any of this with perfect grace. I staggered. I stumbled. But I picked up a journal. I wrote out every fear, every doubt, every question I didn't know how to pray. And slowly — not all at once, but slowly — Romans 8:26 began to make sense to me in a way it never had before. The Spirit interceding through my wordless groans. Because I didn't always have words. I still don't sometimes. But He knew. He always knew what I meant.

I began speaking life over myself deliberately, the way I teach my clients to do.

*Brittany, you are enough. Even now. Especially now. Your body did not fail you. God did not forget you. Not even here. Not even in this valley.*

The lie of *less than* only grows in the dark. So, I kept shining light on it, through journaling, through worship, through thanksgiving even when thanksgiving felt like a stretch. I kept shining light until the lie couldn't find a corner to hide in.

My mind kept drifting back to the years before marriage – how certain I had been, at one point, that partnership simply wasn't in God's plan for me. I remembered the resignation that had quietly settled in my chest back then, the way I mourned a dream I believed would never come. And then, when I surrendered the search entirely to God's will, love arrived.

If marriage came in the fullness of His time, I reasoned, could He not bring children in His own set time too? Was my timeline more important than the masterpiece He was still painting – in colors I hadn't even seen yet?

I began to surrender again. The way I had before. My prayers grew gentler. More honest. Less *give me this now* and more *give me the strength to wait well.* I asked for clarity. I asked for peace. And I asked – perhaps most importantly – *why* something so good and seemingly simple for others continued to elude us. Not so I could argue with the answer, but so I could understand it.

My marriage, through all of this, had quietly become a safe haven. Strengthened not in spite of the struggle but *because* of it. We had a principle we returned to every time frustration crept in through the back door.

"*We're not enemies. We're teammates. We are in this together.*"

Those words built a shelter around our hearts. Every time the world tried to push us apart, we moved closer. We drew battle lines against the problem; never against each other. There is a particular grace in a marriage that refuses to turn inward and cannibalize itself during seasons of pain. I am grateful, to this day, that ours chose a different way.

By months eight, nine, I gave myself away. Not in defeat. Not in bitter resignation. I handed the timing to God along with my plans, my expectations, and the quiet calendar I'd been keeping in the margins of my heart. I let my focus shift to gratitude for what was already present. The marriage that was blooming. The life already being built.

If you are reading this from inside your own season of gut-wrenching waiting, if you are a woman quietly crying out for something your heart aches for so deeply you can barely name it… I see you. I was you. I know the secrecy. I know the shame. I have been the woman half-curled on the edge of a bed, one hand pressed to my mouth so nobody hears me pray words I wasn't even sure I believed would be answered.

There are no quick words for hope tested by longing. There is only this gentle reminder: you are not alone, and what you feel is not your fault, and it is not your failure.

I can't promise it gets easier in a straight line. I can't paint over how hard it truly is. But I can tell you that you are not defined by what your body can or cannot do. Sometimes, rising from the ashes means sifting through them (hands blackened by everything you have survived), and still finding something worth saving.

Our waiting taught us patience. It taught us trust. It taught us the kind of unity that only forms under pressure. We believed that once the waiting was over, the hardest part would be behind us.

But life had a way of showing us that sometimes, the real storm begins after the very first drop of rain.

The real storms were still ahead.

And they came, quickly, without announcement, without mercy.

# Self-Reflection

1. Write about a time when comparison to others robbed you of joy. How can you guard your heart better today?

2. What social media images or voices stir pain in you, and how can you curate your space to nurture healing instead?

3. Recall a season when God seemed silent. How did you respond, and what did you learn about Him in the silence?

4. If you could tell your younger self one thing about waiting, what wisdom would you offer her?

5. Write about a moment when you felt angry with God. What did that honesty open up inside you?

______________________________________________

______________________________________________

______________________________________________

______________________________________________

6. Think of a time someone who loves you said something that hurt more than they realized. What did it stir in you, and what boundaries might help protect your peace going forward?

______________________________________________

______________________________________________

______________________________________________

______________________________________________

7. What small practices (journaling, worship, thanksgiving) helped you resist the lie of being "less than"?

______________________________________________

______________________________________________

______________________________________________

______________________________________________

***Want to go deeper with your reflection?*** *After you complete this chapter's journal prompts, you can choose to share your answers privately with me. With your consent, your story may be included anonymously in a future devotional sequel.*

NOTES

..... / .... / ......

S M T W T F S

*Take a breath. What else do you need to release before turning the page?*

SPEAK THIS OVER YOURSELF

# I'm not forgotten. No! I'm not forsaken. I'm not what my ashes say, I am. I am enough. Even now. Especially now.

***Heavenly Father,***

*You already know the ache I carry; the one I don't always have words for. The months that turned without an answer. The hope I built quietly, only to grieve quietly when it didn't come. I won't pretend I haven't been angry. I won't pretend my faith has never flickered. But even here, in my empty places, I choose You. Even here, I will find my joy in You. Remind me that I am not forgotten; that You are not withholding, but preparing. Give me the grace to hand You my timeline and my expectations. Do what only You can do, Lord; in Your time, and in Your way.* ***In Jesus' name, Amen.***

# VI

# ASHES IN MY WOMB

*"Instead of your shame you will receive double, and instead of disgrace people will shout with joy over your inheritance..."*
*– Isaiah 61:7 (ISV)*

November means something different to everybody. But for me, there is one particular November – the November of 2021 – that is permanently written on my heart. I can still see it so clearly. My husband and I were spending an ordinary weekend together in Ghana; sweeping, picking up laundry, completing our weekend housecleaning tasks so that we could enjoy the afternoon outdoors by the beach. The sunlight was coming in through the windows, and everything felt normal. Peaceful, even.

And then, out of nowhere, I felt something. A strange little pain in my abdomen. Familiar, but off. Like something was gently insisting that I pay attention.

I slipped away to the bathroom; not making a big deal about it, just following that quiet inner nudge that I've learned, over time, not to argue with. Up on the top shelf sat my little stash of home pregnancy tests. That wasn't anything new. We had been trying for months by that point, riding that rollercoaster of hope and heartbreak that so many women know all too well. So, my hands moved almost on autopilot. I took the test, sat down, pulled out my phone, and waited, doing my best to feel nothing, to expect nothing.

But when I looked down and saw two lines, clear as day, something in me went completely still.

*Is this real?*

I turned that stick over in my hands like looking at it from a new angle would tell me something different. There was a rush of excitement — of course there was — but I wouldn't let myself fully grab onto it. My heart had already learned the hard way just how much it costs to hope without a guard up.

I sat there for a moment, wrestling with whether to tell him right then or wait until we could see a doctor. But here we were, thousands of miles away from family, from everything familiar. If this was real, I was going to need him right there with me no matter what came next. So, I called him in.

He looked at that stick with the most confused expression on his face (God, it still makes me smile), until I explained, "It's a pregnancy test. It says positive."

And y'all, his whole face changed. His smile just lit up the entire room.

"*I told you*", he said, eyes shining. "*God would make it happen for us.*"

That was him, every single time. So certain. So anchored. And I loved him deeply for it. But even wrapped in the warmth of his joy, I couldn't quite step all the way in. I whispered that it was too early to celebrate; that so many things can cause a positive result. I needed to know for sure.

A couple of days later, we walked to the small clinic near our home. It was a simple waiting room; quiet, a little uncertain, the kind of space where you sit with your hands folded and your prayers silent. I lay on the exam table while the technician moved the sonogram wand across my belly, squinting at the screen. My husband sat in the corner, waiting patiently for something to confirm what we were hoping for.

Her words, when they came, were gentle. Clinical.

"*It's showing a pregnancy, about six weeks. But I'm not seeing the fetal pole just yet.*"

The fetal pole. That's the first visible sign that an embryo has begun to form; the first thing they look for when life is starting to take shape. She said it could just be too early. She said to come back in a couple of weeks.

Her tone was calm. Almost reassuring. But I had read enough and seen enough to know what it means when you don't see what you're supposed to see. My heart understood what my mind wasn't quite ready to say out loud. Still, I held onto hope, because faith has always been the anchor in my story.

My husband carried that hope like he was born to hold it. He was always the one who saw bumps in the road and called them temporary. "*Everything's gonna be fine,*" he'd tell me with that steady, unshakeable conviction. "*Don't worry.*"

Inside, though? I was a tangle of sadness and questions I couldn't silence. I tried not to let it show. I tried to keep things as normal as they could be. But in those quiet moments, my mind kept coming back to that sonogram printout the technician had handed us before we left. My husband held it like a promise. I held it like a question mark.

I couldn't stop looking at it. My fingers traced the edges over and over again, my eyes searching every blurry pixel for something — anything — that hadn't been found yet. I took a photo and sent it to one of my closest friends living in the States. She'd been through motherhood four times. If anyone would be honest with me, it was her.

"*Does this look right to you?*" I texted.

Her response was exactly what I needed — full of that warm, practical wisdom she always carries. "*It could just be too early. Don't worry. Keep praying, keep believing, and go back like they said.*"

I tucked those words and that sonogram away and tried to release the anxiety's grip on me. Tried.

But the waiting was unbearable. A quiet dread followed me everywhere, whispering *what if* in every idle moment. Finally, instead of sitting in that uncertainty for weeks more, I listened to the deeper instinct inside me, the one that said *go home*. I booked a flight back to the States, hoping that seeing my own doctor, in familiar surroundings, would bring some kind of clarity.

I arrived in mid-December, carrying jet lag and something far heavier; weeks of held breath. My doctor in the States was the kind of steady, seasoned presence you want in those moments. I handed over the sonogram from the clinic in Ghana and explained the whole journey that had brought me through his door.

*"I'm not sure if there's anything viable,"* I told him quietly, *"but I needed to see for myself what's going on."*

My body still hadn't caught up to what I feared. My symptoms were unchanged. My heart was braced but still aching to hold onto hope just a little longer.

We did another sonogram. I watched the screen this time with steady eyes, like if I just stayed calm enough, the news might be softer. I already knew what I was about to hear.

*"There's nothing there, right?"* I asked, quietly, before he could speak.

He was careful and kind. It wasn't that there was *nothing,* but the growth wasn't what it should be. The meaning was clear: the pregnancy was not viable.

*"You miscarried,"* he said gently.

And somehow, I was ready for it. I had spent days and nights mentally preparing for those words, wrapping my mind around the possibility one layer at a time. So, when they came, I just nodded. *"Okay."*

I searched his face for answers, for *why.* He told me, with practiced gentleness, that what I'd experienced was common. That there was nothing I had done. Nothing I could have done differently to prevent it.

*"This type of miscarriage happens often. We don't necessarily know why. But it doesn't mean you can't carry children or have children."*

I tried to let those words sink in, but they seemed to hover just above the wound instead of reaching it. All he could offer in the end was this: *"Continue to try."* No magic answers. No guarantees. Just a gentle push forward into the unknown.

My husband was on the phone, listening as everything unfolded. When the news landed, I saw the sadness flicker across his face, quiet and real. But his optimism found its way back through the cracks the way it always did. He reminded me, gently and with that firm faith of his, that at least now we knew I could get pregnant. That in itself was something. A small, fragile light in the fog. "*Next time,*" he said, "*Next time it will be successful. Next time, a healthy baby.*"

My doctor explained that normally the next step would be a D&C procedure to clear things out. But he hesitated — he was concerned that intervention could leave physical scarring that might create more obstacles down the road. He told me to let nature take its course. To surrender the timeline and trust my body to do what it needed to do.

I left that appointment feeling strangely flat. I expected an emotional storm; the kind that demands answers from God, the kind that brings you to your knees. Instead, there was just... numbness. In the days that followed, I kept replaying his words over and over, as if they might somehow change shape or meaning. But every time, they landed the same: kind, careful, and achingly incomplete.

It was evening when the grief finally found me, choosing my old childhood bedroom as the place where it would make itself known. There's something about the room where you grew up — the faded colors, the old journals, the relics of everything you once believed about your future — that strips away every defense you've built. I sat on the edge of my bed and tried to convince myself I was fine.

I wasn't.

I thought about friends whose lives seemed to be unfolding with such ease. One had gotten married around the same time as me — already welcoming her first child, or close to it. Another, my husband's friend's wife, was glowing with expectancy. Their joy was real, and it wasn't something I begrudged them. But it hurt in a way that had nothing to do with jealousy and everything to do with loss. I just kept asking myself — *why does it feel effortless for them and like a slow climb for me?*

I let myself sit with the questions I'd been tucking away behind my composure. Was my body quietly working against the very thing I'd believed it was capable of? Had God decided that for me, joy would always come braided with pain? I searched for meaning, for some small grace in the middle of not knowing — and instead, I found the tears I'd been holding back for weeks.

I cried. Real, heaving, shoulder-shaking sobs. And I called for my sister.

She filled the doorway and then the bed beside me, and I fell into her the way you only fall into someone who has known you your whole life. Her presence, her scent, the soft sound of her prayers; all of it undid me completely. The words tumbled out of me raw and unfiltered:

*"It seems like anything good I ever want in life never comes easily. I always have to fight for it. Every beautiful thing is born through struggle. Is that just how it's supposed to be for me?"*

She listened. God, she listened the way only a sister can.

And then she gathered me close and she spoke truth over me in the gentlest, most matter-of-fact way.

*"That's not true. You've had so many beautiful things in life that didn't require pain. Don't be too hard on yourself, Brittany. Don't let these feelings pull you under. Don't count yourself out. Don't give in to despair. Just keep praying. Keep believing. Trust that God will work it out in His time."*

That night, wrapped in her arms, I let the tears come — the kind that cleanses, that signals the start of something new.

Then I wiped my face and went back to life as if nothing had happened.

That is the truth of November 2021. I found out I had miscarried; and yet my body kept going as though life were still thriving inside me. For a few more weeks, I carried the loss silently, grieving something the rest of the world couldn't see, while my body stayed stubbornly in the present tense. It wasn't until January 2022 that my body finally let go of what I had already been mourning since December.

Through all of it, I prayed. Quiet, almost secret prayers that filled my days and colored my nights. I whispered them as I prepared to work, under my breath in lines at the grocery store, and louder, more desperate, as I sank into bed. I pleaded for a miracle. I asked God to turn my sorrow around, to make the impossible possible. And every cramp, every pang sent my heart spinning: *Is this it? Or is this grace?*

Then one day, while I was working, in a therapy session with a client, everything shifted. The cramps came on sharp and insistent, stripping away whatever denial I'd been holding onto. My body had finally caught up to a truth my soul had been carrying for weeks. I knew what was happening even before the pain forced my hand to my abdomen and made my breath go shallow. When I started vomiting later that night, barely able to stand, my mother and sister – my two quiet anchors – came and supported me. The pain became too much to bear at home and so, we drove, early morning to the hospital.

The nurses came in. They gave me something for the pain and nausea, small mercies in a moment that felt anything but merciful. By dawn, I was home again. Mind still rigid. It all felt almost redundant, like my heart had already done the work of letting go weeks ago, and my body had just now gotten the message.

After the miscarriage, once again, the world felt like it was holding up a mirror to everything I had lost. Social media was the worst. Bright nurseries, soft cheeks, tiny fingers curled around a mother's thumb; everywhere I looked, someone was celebrating what I was grieving. And it wasn't just strangers on a screen. My circle was full of blossoming pregnancies and birth announcements. I wanted to be happy for them – I really did – but happiness felt like a country I didn't have a passport to. I didn't want bitterness to take root. But it was there, and it needed to be acknowledged.

There were moments closer to home that cut even deeper. I can still hear my mother's voice, casual, unsuspecting, saying, "*So and so had her baby.*" And I remember looking at her, anger rising quietly behind my eyes. Did she not know? Or had she just forgotten what I was still carrying? I didn't say anything. I let the silence stretch. My pain was invisible to her, hidden beneath the everyday flow of life. She meant well. But even the most well-meaning words can press right into the softest parts of you.

What I learned in those weeks was how isolating grief can be. The world expects you to return to yourself, to resume the performance of normalcy. My family saw me smile, heard me laugh, noticed when I went back to work – and assumed that meant I was healed. But deep down, I was aching for someone to understand or share in the sorrow.

The truth is, I felt alone. So, I looked outward, sat up late at my computer, searching through the vast, anonymous world of the internet for voices like mine. YouTube became a lifeline. I watched women who had walked this road before me, women whose stories were cracked open and honest and somehow exactly what I needed. Their words reached right through the screen and touched something I hadn't been able to name. Their hope helped me find my own.

I wrote to women on blogs; strangers, really, but sisters in experience. One response, from someone halfway across the country, wrapped around my heart in a way I didn't expect. Simple, kind, honest. Through her words, I found a small, quiet permission to hope again. Sometimes it really is the voice of another survivor (not a professional, not a poet), that finally lets us breathe.

Journaling became another refuge. Each morning, I poured my hopes and hurts into the pages of my notebook, saying to God the things I couldn't say out loud: the longing, the ache, the desperate wish to be a mother. There was something holy in that. Even when my prayers felt unanswered. Even when the pages gathered more tears than ink. By naming my desires to God, I slowly began to recognize them as part of my story, not something to bury or deny.

I began reading the Word with fresh eyes. Verses about hope and desire became something I could lean on. And I came to believe, deeply and stubbornly, that this longing inside me, to nurture, to bring life, was not placed there to be snatched away. That if God put that desire in my heart, He intended to fulfill it. My faith began to shift from wishing to *trusting*. Not in the outcome I could see, but in the process I couldn't.

That shift, from focusing on the wound to focusing on the possibility, is where my healing began in earnest.

How long did healing take? That question found me again and again. I wish I could give it a clean answer — a receipt stamped *six months, all done*. But healing doesn't work like that. It came slowly, in trembling steps. Some days the anger still pushed its way back in, threading doubt and self-pity through my thoughts. But I learned to let it ebb and flow without letting it consume me.

There were moments when my prayers were full of hurt. When I was ricocheting off the walls of my own disbelief, spilling raw, unfiltered emotion at God's feet. I used to think that coming to Him in confusion and anger was somehow shameful. That He only wanted my praise when I had it together. But loss has a way of burning through pretense. And in that scorched ground, I found something more real: an invitation to come exactly as I am.

I shook my fists at God. I wept and questioned. And then the very next day, I'd find myself whispering prayers for peace, inching back toward the grace I'd tried to push away. To anyone watching from the outside, that probably looked like a contradiction. But I've come to see it for what it was: the sacred rhythm of being human and being a child of God. We are given the full spectrum of emotion, and we are meant to bring every bit of it to the One who truly understands.

God does not ask us to scrub our feelings clean before we come to Him. He wants our honesty. Our vulnerability is the very thing that invites His comfort.

It was only when I stopped performing and allowed myself to come undone before Him (voicing my bitterness, my shame, my secret fears), that I actually received the comfort I'd been desperately needing. My defenses came down. I laid the debris of my soul right there at His feet. And it was in that place of brokenness and honesty that I heard Him say, *This pain is real, but it is not forever. This season will not define all your days. You are not alone. You are not forgotten. My grace is sufficient for you. My strength is made perfect in your weakness.*

I know now that if I had tried to paste over that pain with distractions or numbed it with empty comfort, nothing inside me would have truly changed. The ache would have stayed, quietly corroding my hope from the inside. It was only through God's embrace that I was able to lay down the weight of embarrassment and hopelessness I'd been carrying. Without Him, I might still be under it.

But God is faithful just as He promises. His character is kindness and restoration, not condemnation. He invites us, again and again, to come near. To let Him bind what shame would try to destroy. I have learned to trust that bringing my full self; bruised, messy, completely authentic, is what He desires from me. That is where transformation lives. That is where hope takes root.

Through this season, a particular scripture became a steady light for me; the promise of Isaiah 61:7:

"*Instead of your shame you will receive a double portion, and instead of disgrace you will rejoice in your inheritance.*"

To the woman holding this book. The one whose heart is quietly racing right now. The one who is reading these words in a place where she doesn't have to pretend. I want you to know this: you are not alone. And you are not to blame.

I write this for you. The woman reading in silence, tucked away somewhere the world can't see the shadows that have settled inside you. I see you, because I have *been* you. I have worn that heavy coat of shame and confusion, asking over and over again, "*Is this my fault?*"

And the answer — every time — is *no.*

Life sometimes hands us burdens that make no sense. Burdens with origins too tangled, too hidden for easy answers. When I finally gave myself permission to research, to ask questions, to voice my pain out loud, I learned that these struggles are far from rare. Women everywhere have walked this path before us, for reasons too complex for any simple explanation. I wish someone had stood beside me then and said plainly: *Sometimes life just happens. Not because you are wrong. Not because you are broken. But because you are alive.*

There is a strange and quiet freedom in accepting how much is out of our control. We have been taught that control is power. But there is a different kind of power in surrender, a gentle, holy power in releasing what was never ours to carry alone.

Your struggle is not evidence of your failure. It is a chapter; one you did not ask to write, but one that can still find a redemptive ending.

In my darkest hours, my own thoughts became my greatest enemy. I said things to myself I would never say to another person. I asked my body *why* it couldn't just work. With every question, my spirit shrank smaller. But healing began. Not with answers, not with diagnoses, but with the words I slowly, stubbornly learned to speak over myself. Even when they felt like a lie. Even when my voice shook.

I stood in front of the mirror, eyes red from too many sleepless nights, and I said: *You are enough as you are. Your body is doing its best. This is not your fault.*

Please, hear me when I tell you this:

- Speak to yourself as you would speak to someone you love deeply because you deserve that same compassion.
- Let go of shame's hollow insistence. You have carried it long enough.
- When the emotion surges, feel it, but do not let it convince you that you are less than. You are so much more, even in your lowest valley.
- Seek knowledge. Seek help. Choose hope. Knowledge is armor, but hope is your fire.

Our stories do not have to end in the ashes. There is life after this kind of hurt; gentle, fierce, and true. And every word you speak over yourself, every act of kindness toward your own heart, is another brick in the foundation of your comeback.

Be tender with yourself. You are not defective. You are not to blame. Your worth is unshakeable. Trust in the slow, hopeful work of loving yourself through pain. Speak light over your shadows, you *will* find your way again.

I believed these words myself. And in that season, they carried me.

They carried me through a chapter that taught me how to grieve quietly. How to keep moving while my heart held more than it was built to hold. How to function in a world that did not pause for my pain.

What I didn't know yet was that everything I was learning, every ounce of endurance, every hard-won layer of faith, would soon be required of me...

Again.

# Self-Reflection

1. What part of Brittany's story in this chapter resonated most deeply with you, and why do you think it touched that place in your heart?

2. Which moment in her story felt most familiar to your own experience of loss, disappointment, or waiting?

3. When Brittany described carrying grief quietly while life moved on, where have you felt that same pressure to appear "fine"?

4. How has comparison to others fueled envy, and how can you redirect that energy into faith?

5. Where have comparison or other people's joy intensified your grief, even when you wanted to be happy for them?

______________________________________________

______________________________________________

______________________________________________

______________________________________________

6. What emotions surfaced for you as you read this chapter: sadness, anger, fear, numbness, relief... what might they be revealing?

______________________________________________

______________________________________________

______________________________________________

______________________________________________

7. What emotions did you feel toward God that you were afraid to admit: anger, confusion, disappointment, resentment?

______________________________________________

______________________________________________

______________________________________________

______________________________________________

***Want to go deeper with your reflection?** After you complete this chapter's journal prompts, you can choose to share your answers privately with me. With your consent, your story may be included anonymously in a future devotional sequel.*

# NOTES

..... / .... / ......

S M T W T F S

*There's no rush here, friend. What more is God speaking over you?*

SPEAK THIS OVER YOURSELF

# I am not defective. I am not defeated. Life may bend me, break me, bring me to my knees — but my worth? My worth does not move.

***Heavenly Father,***

*I come to You with all of it; the waiting, the ache, the questions, and the silence that some days feels unbearable. I won't pretend I have it all together, Lord, because You already know I don't. Teach me to see this season differently. Give me a grateful heart for what You've already placed in my hands, even as I trust You for what is still to come. And on the days my strength gives out, please hold me close. Remind me that Your arms are steady even when mine are not. I trust You, Lord. Even now.* ***In Jesus' name, Amen.***

# VII
# ASHES OF A BROKEN HEART

*"The Lord is close to the brokenhearted and saves those who are crushed in spirit."*
*– Psalm 34:18*

Eric Sarfo entered this world on April 11, 1988, in the golden-hearted pulse of Accra, Ghana—a city that celebrates life with the rhythm of highlife music and the roar of Black Stars victories. His story began in a country I had only read about in glossy travel magazines and church mission newsletters, long before I ever saw its red earth with my own eyes or felt the weight of Kente cloth draped across my shoulders.

By the time I met him, Ghana had already carved its shapes and rhythms into his soul: the cadence of the streets filled with market women balancing headloads, the easy laughter of young boys chasing footballs through dusty neighborhoods, the steady hum of aunties cooking Ghana Jollof, while also correcting, advising, or teasing someone at the same time.

Eric was raised between those sounds, largely in the care of his grandmother, while his father served in the military and his mother traveled back and forth to the States, working to provide in ways that required her absence. I imagine that tension (between presence and distance, between stability and sacrifice), taught him early how to hold both longing and gratitude in the same hand.

He grew up as the third child among a constellation of siblings: two older brothers, a younger sister, and others from his father's side. The house was never empty, never quiet in the way Western homes sometimes are. There were always footsteps, voices, arguments that turned into laughter, and laughter that dissolved into silence when someone's feelings were bruised. In that swirl of energy, Eric learned to be both participant and observer. People remember him as the boy who played sports and ran with his friends, the one who always seemed to be in the middle of the action and yet somehow carried a softness that set him apart.

He was popular, yet gentle; reserved, yet deeply connected. I like to think that even then, God was crafting in him the kind of heart that would one day make me feel safe just by being in the same room.

When I speak about Eric, I almost always start with his heart, because that was the part of him that introduced itself first, long before any grand romantic gesture or carefully curated words. He had a way of moving through the world with his hands open. If someone needed money, he gave it. If someone needed time, he carved it out. If someone needed encouragement, he poured from a well that seemed endless, at least to the outside world.

There were moments, especially once we got married, when I would gently tug him aside and talk about boundaries, about what it means to love people without sacrificing yourself at the altar of their expectations. He listened, he heard me, but the next time the phone rang with a need, his instinct was still to say, "*How can I help?*" He saw the good in people long after their "true colors" had been on display. Where I saw red flags, he often saw wounded hearts.

But it would be too simple, too unfair, to paint him as naïve. Eric watched people carefully. He was not loud in his discernment, but it was there, simmering under the surface. His quietness often fooled people who thought silence meant emptiness, yet when he chose to speak, about a situation, a person, a decision; his words carried the weight of someone who had been paying attention all along.

In so many ways, he embodied what I grew up hearing described as the fruit of the Spirit: gentle and kind, forgiving past what seemed reasonable, patient when others had long given up. He was not perfect, but he was sincere, and in a world that often rewards performance over authenticity, that sincerity felt like a rare, holy thing.

People loved him. That part of his story is simple and true. Friends, cousins, coworkers, neighbors, no matter who I asked, the responses sounded like variations of the same song: *"Eric is kind." "Eric is generous." "Eric is wise."* It is a strange thing to share your husband with the world in that way, to know that the man you love most is also the man so many lean on. Yet for me, it only deepened my love, because I got to see what they saw. And then, in the quiet places, I also got to see what they did not.

There were nights when the door closed and the visitors were gone that I saw a different side of him. I saw the toll it took to always be the strong one, the giver, the problem-solver. He rarely complained, but there were moments when the hurt slipped out, when he would sit on the edge of the bed or the couch, eyes distant, and I could feel the weight of his disappointment in people who had taken and taken and never thought to pour back. He wore a kind of emotional armor in public, a shield that kept his vulnerability tucked away. With me, that shield loosened. Behind closed doors, I watched him wrestle with what it means to be deeply loving in a world that does not always know how to love back.

His faith was like that too: quiet and steady, less about speeches and more about the choices he made when no one was watching. From a young age, belief in God had been planted in him like a seed, and though life sometimes pulled him away from church buildings and organized routines, the root never left.

He knew Scripture. He respected it. He tried, in his imperfect human way, to live by it. If you were looking for the loud, always-at-the-mic kind of Christian, you might have missed him. But if you paid attention to how he treated people, to the mercy he extended, to the patience he showed, you would have seen the fingerprints of God all over his life.

I had my own complicated journey with faith. I knew what it meant to love God and also to question Him, to show up on Sunday while silently dragging around bruises from the week before. By the time I met Eric, I had already carried my share of disappointments, relationships that promised safety but delivered pain, dreams that crumbled, prayers that seemed to bounce off the ceiling. There was a part of me that was tired, another part that was still stubbornly hopeful.

When Eric and I began talking seriously, it was his faith, even in its subdued expression, that caught my attention and refused to let go. It wasn't perfect; it was real. That mattered to me more than any title or position. I needed a partner whose relationship with God was not just a performance, but an anchor. In him, I found that.

His faith showed up most clearly when life stripped us down to the bone. When we walked through the valley and the ache of trying to conceive and facing miscarriage, my own faith shook like a house in a storm.

There were days when I felt swallowed by questions and grief I was almost ashamed to name. In those moments, Eric became a steady presence. He didn't always have the right words (sometimes there are no right words), but he had this quiet, almost childlike trust that God would *"work everything out for us."* He was not blind to our sorrow; he just refused to let it be the final sentence. That steady trust held us when my own belief felt thin and shredded.

We met, physically, in Ghana, but the story started long before my plane ticket was booked. A mutual friend from church, who had met Eric years earlier while studying abroad in China, and I would sit and talk about traveling to Africa. We would scroll through photos, talk about countries we wanted to visit. When she finally reached out to Eric about visiting Ghana, he responded with the warmth that would later feel so familiar. He told her Ghana would be a wonderful first stop on the continent; open, friendly, a place that knew how to welcome. He offered to host us, not as some grand gesture, but because that's who he was.

I arrived in Ghana thinking I was just going on a trip with a friend. I left with my life changed. In those first days, Eric was simply our host: tall, quiet, hospitable in a way that felt almost effortless.

My first impression of him was that he was like a gentle giant, a big teddy bear walking around in human form, taking care of logistics, making sure we were safe, making sure we ate. As the trip went on, our conversations deepened. We talked about faith, family, purpose. There was something in the way he saw the world that resonated with the deepest parts of me.

By the end of the trip, we exchanged numbers. When I returned to the States, what could have been a polite, occasional check-in turned into a daily rhythm. Morning, afternoon, evening, if there was a spare pocket of time, we found a way to fill it with conversation. We laughed, we dreamed, we challenged each other. Somewhere in those calls, I felt my heart do that dangerous, holy thing: begin to hope again.

Six months later, I returned to Ghana, this time by myself. That trip moved us from unspoken understanding into explicit commitment.

We made it "official," not with fireworks or dramatic declarations, but with the quiet certainty of two people who had already been building something real. I would not say that there was one single moment when I "knew" he was the one, the way movies sometimes portray it. Instead, there were hundreds of small moments: the way he spoke life into me when I doubted myself, the ways he looked past my exterior and reached for my heart, the alignment of our values, our shared desire to build a family centered in God, to live lives that meant something beyond ourselves. It was in those cumulative moments that the thought formed and grew: *"This man could be my husband."*

The man became my husband!

What I loved most about Eric was how large his heart was and how unashamed he was to let it lead him. He did not let his friends or cultural expectations dictate how he showed up as a husband. In spaces where men were sometimes encouraged to be distant, emotionally guarded, or controlling, he chose a different path. He was attentive, affectionate, willing to listen and adjust. He did not always get it right, but he was always willing to try again. There was a quiet courage in that, a refusal to be squeezed into a mold that didn't fit him.

With him, I felt safe, in the kind of way that makes your nervous system sigh in relief. I never found myself questioning whether he loved me or whether he was being genuine. Around him, I could exhale. I could be soft where the world had taught me to be hard. I could lay down the performance and be fully, unapologetically myself, including the parts of me that still trembled from old wounds.

There was one moment, early on, that still makes me smile. We were at Labadi Beach, one of Ghana's beloved stretches of shoreline. To get from the parking area to the actual beach, you have to take a small boat. The water was choppy, the boat rocking just enough to rattle my sense of balance. Without thinking, I wrapped my arm around him to steady myself. It was instinctual, not symbolic, but when I think back on it now, it feels like a small prophecy: this reaching out to him when the ground (or in this case, the water) felt unstable.

When we got off the boat, he helped me down, hands firm and gentle at the same time. Looking back, I think that was the first time we both quietly acknowledged that something deeper was happening between us, even if we didn't yet have the words.

Eric showed love in details that might have looked ordinary to someone standing far away. He made me coffee in the mornings because he knew how much it mattered to me to start the day with that familiar warmth.

When I moved to Ghana, he paid attention to the foods and comforts I missed from home and would show up with my favorite snacks whenever he could find them, small offerings of normalcy in a season when everything else felt foreign. He noticed what flavors made my eyes light up, what drinks made me nostalgic, what comforts eased the homesickness that crept in when I least expected it. His love did not depend on grand gestures; it lived in those small, faithful acts that whispered, *"I see you. I'm paying attention. I'm trying to make this easier."*

Our ordinary days together were simple and sacred all at once. We would go on walks or runs around the neighborhood, trying to keep our bodies healthy and our minds clear. We cooked breakfast, sometimes talking, sometimes just moving around each other in a comfortable silence that only comes when two people know each other well.

We prayed together, read our Bibles together, worshipped together. Then, the day would separate us: he would go out to run his business, and I would log in to my job, operating on a different time zone. I often worked later into the evening, and he would come home to dinner already prepared. If we weren't too tired by the end of the night, we would curl up with a movie or a show, talk about the day, and then drift off to sleep.

On the weekends, we tried to get out as much as life allowed: dinners in the city, outings with friends, staycations at different resorts around Ghana. We didn't travel outside the country as a married couple, but we made Ghana our shared playground.

We dreamed, too—big, layered dreams. We dreamed of having children, of watching them run through the house with Ghanaian and American roots intertwined. We dreamed of starting a life together in the States, of standing in my parents' kitchen with Eric beside me, finally able to touch all the people he had only met over video calls. We talked about building businesses together, creating generational wealth that could ripple beyond our lifetimes.

We explored ideas: owning property in Ghana and turning it into an Airbnb, designing and selling clothing with bold African prints in an online boutique. I loved African print. The vibrancy. The joy stitched into every pattern. And those dreams felt like pieces of my heart and his culture woven together.

We also had itineraries written in our hearts: trips to Kenya, to Seychelles, to American cities Eric had only seen in movies. We imagined vacations, anniversaries, and quiet trips just the two of us, holding hands in airports instead of letting them pull us apart. In my mind, our future looked like the dream many married couples share but rarely feel the need to say out loud: work hard, build something, retire at a certain age, enjoy each other, watch grandchildren grow, maybe split time between a home in the States and a vacation house in Ghana.

I did not get to see how that story ended. In May of 2023, before the vacations and the anniversaries and the grandchildren, Eric was taken from me.

When it happened, I was in my apartment in Houston, asleep in a bed that suddenly felt far too big for one person. His death was sudden, at least in the natural sense, but my spirit had felt a tremor weeks before.

Two or three weeks earlier, I'd had a dream, or maybe it was closer to a vision. It was brief, not cinematic, but it left a mark. I saw three men, their backs turned, dressed in black. Eric stood in the middle. A wave of dread washed over me in the dream, thick and heavy, like a shadow that knew my name. When I jolted awake, my heart raced and my body buzzed with anxiety.

I couldn't quite put into words what I had seen, but everything in me knew it was not good. I called him immediately. He answered, his voice with a familiar jovial tone on the other end of the line. I told him I'd had a strange dream but couldn't bring myself to speak the full fear aloud. The idea of naming it felt like signing a contract I had no interest in. He listened, then gently encouraged me to pray. We prayed God's protection over his life and tried to move on, but part of me tucked that dream away, unsettled.

A month before his passing, I had flown to Ghana to celebrate his birthday, as we did every year. We laughed, ate, and soaked in the sweetness of being together. When it was time to leave, we stood at the airport, both a little tired of that now-familiar ache that comes with parting. One of the last things we said to each other was, "*This will be the last time we have to separate at the airport. Next time, we're leaving together.*" I believed that with all my heart. I did not yet know that our "last time" together had already happened.

The day he died, Houston's sky mirrored the heaviness I felt in my chest before I even knew why. The morning was cloudy and gray, the kind of day that never seems to fully wake up. We spoke on the phone, like we always did. He told me he was going to visit a friend who had just had their first child. It was nothing unusual, just another thread in the fabric of our routine.

After that, the day moved on. He went about his plans; I went about mine. We didn't talk as much as we usually did – he was out with friends, living the ordinary kind of day that gives you no reason to hold on tighter. The last time we spoke, he told me he was heading home and would call once he got there. Fifteen, maybe thirty minutes at most. I didn't think twice about it. I went on with my evening, waiting for a call that felt routine, the kind you don't even realize you're waiting for until the silence stretches too long.

I went to sleep trying not to spiral, trying not to let my mind wander to the places it had no business going. It's nothing, I told myself. He's probably tired. He'll call in the morning. But somewhere beneath the reassurance, something in me wouldn't settle. And then, around 1 a.m., my body jolted awake. Not from a sound, not from a dream, but from something deeper. A knowing that lived below logic. My spirit felt it before my mind could name it.

I turned over. My phone was already ringing.

It was his friend. And in the seconds before a single word was spoken, I already knew. The news, when it came, felt like words spoken underwater: distant, distorted, impossible to fully absorb. My mind could not wrap itself around the sentence: '*Eric is gone.*' Thirty minutes. That was all it was supposed to be. It became the rest of my life. The first emotion was disbelief, then a shock so absolute it seemed to numb everything else

I called his phone, anyway, fully expecting him to pick up and laugh at some misunderstanding. He didn't answer. I called my mother, no answer. I called my sister; she picked up, and the words tumbled out of me. She went to my mom, and from there, the news spread like a slow, cruel fire.

I remember standing in my apartment, the room suddenly unfamiliar. It felt like it had expanded, as if the walls had receded and I was standing in an empty shell. The air felt colder; the silence sounded louder. I have never felt that particular hollowness before or since. It was as if everything that had once given the room meaning; our conversations, our dreams, the way I paced while talking to him on the phone, had been yanked out, leaving only space.

At first, I was not angry at God. I was confused, disoriented, walking around inside a story that made no sense.

Anger came later, creeping in once the initial numbness began to thaw. It wasn't just anger that he died; it was anger that this particular fear, one I had carried quietly for reasons I didn't fully understand, had come to pass. I had often worried about losing my partner, imagined the possibility in ways I could never entirely explain. To see that fear become reality felt like standing in the middle of my worst nightmare and being told to find something good in it.

I wrestled with questions I still don't fully have answers for: *Why did this happen? How did it happen? Why wasn't he protected?*

*Was this something that had always been written, a line in a story I never got to read ahead of time?*

My faith, once a steady hum beneath my life, trembled. It did not disappear, but it cracked.

The first week after his death was less about living and more about surviving breath to breath. Eating felt like a chore I had no energy for. Food turned to dust in my mouth. Sleep was scattered, shallow. Waking up felt like being pulled against my will into a reality I didn't want. The simplest tasks; showering, answering a text, sitting up, felt like climbing mountains. The first "without him" that cut me deeply was my birthday. Birthdays had been something we shared and celebrated together. That year, the day itself felt like a betrayal, like time had the audacity to keep moving when my life had stopped.

Behind closed doors, grief looked different from the composed snapshots people sometimes see at funerals or church services. It looked like me lying in bed, staring at the ceiling, the weight of the world sitting on my chest. It looked like silent tears soaking into my pillow and, on other days, loud, guttural cries that came from somewhere deeper than my lungs, sounds I didn't know my body could make.

Sometimes grief came out as worship: me singing through tears, lifting songs about God's goodness when my life felt anything but good. I read my Bible like a starving person, not because I always understood or agreed with what I read, but because I had nowhere else to go for words bigger than my pain.

As time passed, grief shapeshifted. It became the awkwardness of re-learning how to be alone, not just physically but emotionally. I had to figure out what mornings looked like without our daily phone calls, what evenings felt like without our debriefs, what it meant to plan a future when the person I had planned it with was no longer here. Slowly, painfully, I began to let God occupy some of those spaces. I asked Him to be what my husband could no longer be for me, at least in this lifetime: comforter, companion, confidant.

For the first three months, I was rarely physically alone. My family held me up. My parents, my sister, my close friends, my childhood pastor. They checked on me, sat with me, made sure I ate when they could coax me into it. I was not lonely in the geographical sense. But there is a loneliness that comes from being the only one carrying a particular kind of grief. None of them had buried a husband. None of them had picked out a future with someone and then watched that future crumble without warning. In that sense, yes, I felt profoundly alone. Surrounded, yet solitary in my pain.

My body responded to grief by shutting down. My appetite vanished. I lost weight quickly, not out of intention but out of inability to consume anything beyond the bare minimum. My mind felt foggy, my nervous system frayed, as if my body was constantly bracing for another impact even when nothing was happening. Joy became something distant, almost theoretical. I laughed sometimes, but even in those moments, there was a heaviness underneath, like a weight tied to my ribcage that refused to be shaken loose.

And yet, even there, God found me.

He met me in dreams, some of them startlingly vivid, where His presence felt less like an idea and more like a person in the room. He spoke into my spirit about comfort, about support, about how He would carry me through what felt impossible. He met me in worship, too. When I lifted my voice, even weakly, there were moments when His presence felt tangible, wrapping around me like a blanket.

Those encounters did not erase my pain, but they softened it at the edges. Slowly, I began to believe that the promise of turning mourning into joy was not just an abstract verse for other people, it was for me, too.

Certain Scriptures became my anchors. Ecclesiastes 3, with its rhythm of "a time to" and "a time to," reminded me that life is made of seasons and that none of them last forever, not even the ones that feel endless.

Verses like Psalm 34:18 and Psalm 147:3 told me that God was close to the brokenhearted, that He heals the broken in spirit. Matthew 5:4 promised that those who mourn would be comforted. Psalm 116 reminded me that God hears our cries and bends low to listen. I did not always *feel* these truths, but I held onto them like a lifeline.

Grief, over time, taught me something profound about love. I came to see that deep grief is proof that deep love existed. It is the echo of connection. It is the soul's way of saying, *"This mattered. This person mattered."* We often think we want love without risk, bond without vulnerability, but that's not how it works. If you desire a love that permeates your soul, you must accept that grief will one day tug at its edges, whether through death, distance, or seasons of suffering. In a strange, painful way, my grief for Eric became a testimony to the depth of what we shared. It hurt so much because it had been so real.

There came a moment—quiet, almost hidden—when I realized I would not only survive this loss but somehow, with God's help, learn to live fully again.

That realization came through another dream.

In it, the Lord spoke to my spirit with a clarity I cannot fully explain in words. As I hovered between sleep and waking, I heard Him call me a warrior and tell me He was doing something new. At that time, I felt anything but strong. I felt drained, fragile, certain I had nothing left to give. Those words cut through my exhaustion and planted something inside me, a resolve, a permission to believe that my story did not end in the cemetery.

From that point, I made a quiet agreement with myself and with God: I would honor every emotion that came. I would cry when I needed to cry, rest when I needed to rest, scream when I needed to scream. I would not rush my grieving to make others more comfortable. But I would also listen for His voice when He whispered that a shift was coming, when He gently nudged me to step into the next season. I did not want to become a prisoner of my own pain, living in a room built of memories without ever opening the door to what God might still want to do.

Rebuilding my life did not come with a grand announcement. It started with small, deliberate choices. I found a church, one where I could quietly slip in with my broken heart and not feel like I had to paste on a smile. I began to build new friendships; tiny threads of connection that reminded me community was still possible.

I returned to work, not because I was "over" my grief, but because routine gave my days a frame. I carved out time to sit with God, to let Him minister to me through His Word, through stillness, through tears. Some days I felt like I was walking forward; other days, I felt like I was crawling. Both counted.

In the context of losing Eric, "rising" took on a particular weight. It meant refusing to let the word "widow" become my definition instead of just a chapter of my story. It meant confronting the shame, guilt, and embarrassment I initially felt: questions about what people might assume, what they might whisper, their theories about whether I was ever meant to marry him. It meant choosing vulnerability over hiding, deciding that I would tell this story not as a scandal to be hushed but as a testimony of God's presence in devastation. Rising meant taking my power back by opening my mouth, by writing these words, by allowing God to get glory even from the ashes.

I am not the same woman who boarded a plane years ago to visit a friend in Ghana. I am more spiritually grounded. My discernment has sharpened; I notice things in the spiritual realm that I once brushed aside as intuition or mood. My relationship with the Lord is stronger, more stubborn, less easily shaken.

I still have days when I feel low. Days when I miss Eric so much it feels like the grief is brand new. I still get tired, frustrated, overwhelmed. Being more mature spiritually has not made me less human. But the way I see my life has changed. I feel the urgency of calling now, the importance of doing what God put me on this earth to do.

In this whole process, I discovered—or maybe remembered—a strength I did not fully know I had.

My resilience surprised me, not because I shoved my grief away and pretended I was fine, but because I learned to recognize when it was time to shift. I could sense when a certain level of mourning had run its course, when staying in that emotional space would no longer be healing but would start to stagnate my spirit. That awareness did not mean the grief vanished; it meant I learned to carry it differently. I refused to become a slave to a single season, even one as monumental as losing my husband.

If you are reading this and you have just lost your husband, this is what I would do if we were sitting across from each other right now.

I would first say nothing.

I would let the silence stretch long enough for you to know that I am not here to patch your broken heart with clichés. When the moment felt right, I would tell you that I know, in ways I wish I didn't, something of this pain you're carrying. I would tell you that I am sending you all the empathy, warmth, and prayer my heart can hold. And I would tell you that I am not merely hoping, but believing, that God will comfort you as He comforted me, that He will reveal Himself to you in new ways and give you exactly what you need, in the exact moments you need it.

I would tell you that you may not see any light right now, and that this is okay. The darkness does not mean the light is gone; it simply means it is out of view for the moment. In time, maybe slowly, maybe suddenly, God will allow rays of light to break through again.

You will feel it when that shift comes. You will recognize when the intense, suffocating phase of grief begins to ease, even though the ache may never entirely disappear. One day, you will look back and see a strange, unexpected beauty woven through this dark tapestry.

I would also gently warn you that grief makes us vulnerable, and in that vulnerability, the enemy will try to twist your pain into bitterness, isolation, or unbelief. I would encourage you to cling to God, even if all you can do is whisper His name through tears, even if your only prayer is, "Help."

I would remind you that your grieving process is your own. You do not owe anyone a timeline. The loudest voice you need to listen for in this season is not the voice of friends, family, or society, but the voice of the Lord, who knows the exact pace at which your heart can heal.

That truth carried me through my own darkness.

And I must be honest with you, rising from your ashes does not mean erasing that fire or pretending the burn marks aren't there. It means honoring the scars and yet daring to believe that life can still grow from scorched ground. It means allowing your humanity to breathe, to feel, to question, while still anchoring yourself to the one true God who can hold all of it without flinching.

That is what this chapter of my life has been: a slow, trembling, courageous rise from the ashes of a life I loved, into a future I am still discovering…

And that's where beauty begins!

# Self-Reflection

1. Where in your life have you loved so deeply that losing it felt like losing part of yourself?

2. Have you ever carried anger toward God like a secret you were ashamed to confess? What part of you feared that honesty might cost you faith?

3. Is there a memory that still makes you smile before it makes you weep? What does that memory reveal about the depth of your capacity to love?

4. What questions are you still carrying that you have not fully voiced, even in prayer?

5. Is there a part of your story you have been tempted to hide because it feels too painful or too misunderstood?

6. In what ways has loss attempted to rename you? Widow. Abandoned. Forgotten. Unchosen. What name does God call you instead?

7. When you think about rising, what fears surface? Fear of judgment? Fear of moving on? Fear of forgetting? Fear of hope?

***Want to go deeper with your reflection?*** *After you complete this chapter's journal prompts, you can choose to share your answers privately with me. With your consent, your story may be included anonymously in a future devotional sequel.*

## NOTES

..... / .... / ......

S M T W T F S

*Don't rush past this. What else is on your heart right now?*

SPEAK THIS OVER YOURSELF

# I'm still chosen. Still called. Still covered. Still crowned with grace. Still loved. Still rising.

***Dear Lord,***
*I come to You without pretending. You know the love I carried. You know the loss that followed. You know the questions I have whispered when no one else could hear. Some days I am grieving. Some days I am angry. Some days I do not understand You at all. But I am still here. Thank You for holding me when I could not hold myself together. Teach me how to honor what I have lost without becoming defined by it. Teach me how to heal without guilt. Teach me how to rise without fear. Bind what feels broken. Quiet what feels restless. Strengthen what feels weak. Be near in my mourning. Be good in my confusion. Hold me as I rise. Please Lord.* ***In Jesus' name, Amen.***

# VIII
# BEAUTY FOR ASHES

*"The Spirit of the Lord is upon me because he has anointed me…*
*to bind up the brokenhearted… to comfort all who mourn…*
*to give them beauty for ashes…"*
*– Isaiah 61:1–3*

Those three months after my husband passed are months I will never fully be able to describe to anyone who wasn't there. After hearing the Lord say it was time to shift, that the healing that He needed to do in me could not be done while I was distracted by the presence of others, I retreated. Not to friends, not to family, not to the well-meaning voices that circle a grieving person with advice and casseroles and carefully chosen words.

I retreated to the Lord; wholly, desperately, with nothing left to perform or protect. I shut myself into my apartment with His Word, and I stayed. Three months of worship every single morning. Scripture through the day. Silence where there had once been a life full of another person's presence.

I was not running to other people for advice or for comfort or for validation. I was not calling friends in the middle of the night to be talked down from the edge. I was alone with God, reading His Word, laying myself open before Him and asking Him to show me something, anything, that would help me understand why I was still here and what I was supposed to do next.

And in that season of radical stillness, He spoke.

What He said was not exactly gentle. Some people might hear it and think it sounds cruel. But what the Lord basically told me was: *Look beyond yourself. What you are going through is bigger than just you – it is also for souls connected to your calling.* And as strange as it sounds, that was actually a relief. As someone who has spent most of her professional life pouring into other people, that message landed somewhere deep and true inside me. I have always found purpose in being useful to someone else. The idea that my pain was not pointless (that it was, in fact, a kind of assignment) was exactly the thing I needed to pull my focus from the wound and toward the horizon.

He showed me that my healing journey could become a glimmer of hope for someone else. That the things He helped me survive could reach someone sitting in their own darkness and remind them that survival is possible.

During those three months of isolation, every earthly comfort fell away, drawing me into the ever-comforting arms of the One who knows suffering's depths. There, in profound solitude, with only the Lord's presence, another realization broke like dawn.

It was Scripture.

Not as something I was reading but as something I was standing inside.

“The Spirit of the Lord is upon me because he has anointed me… to bind up the brokenhearted… to comfort all who mourn… to give them beauty for ashes…” (Isaiah 61:1–3).

I had read those words before as prophecy, as promise, as something beautiful meant for someone else. But in that quiet room, they settled on me differently, no longer glittering like a crown but pressing on my heart like a commission. The Spirit who had carried me through grief had never been moving at random; He had been shaping me in the dark. What I once named survival, I began to recognize as preparation. What I assumed was private healing revealed itself as public equipping.

I realized I wasn’t being set apart to suffer; I was being trusted with an assignment.

Hear this truth, friend: the sacred labor God weaves through your sorrow often spills beyond your own borders. Scripture names Him "the Father of compassion and the God of all comfort, who comforts us in all our troubles so that we can comfort those in any trouble with the comfort we ourselves receive from Him." Those lines pulsed through my veins, alive. The comfort, wisdom, resilience He lavished weren’t mine to hoard. They were meant for the next person who would need to borrow my story as a lantern in their own night.

Shifting gaze from self to service unlocked something profound. I was able to step back from my story to see that what I was going through (no matter how consuming) did not define me. It did not dictate my value, nor script my tomorrows. My suffering, I learned, could either overwhelm me or be surrendered to the Lord’s hands as the canvas for a testimony brighter than the pain that inspired it.

Even when my apartment walls closed like a cell, that morning worship (day after relentless day) wove a bridge from my shattered heart to God's boundless wholeness. Psalm 34:18 took flesh in my frailty: "The Lord is close to the brokenhearted," a nearness that shattered grief's lie that I'm utterly alone.

Suddenly, distance grew between me and the story I thought defined me. It was as if I was given the grace to step outside myself for a moment, to see that everything I'd endured might one day become someone else's encouragement. The Lord whispered, "This experience is not yours to hoard; it is your offering for souls unseen, hungry for the comfort your story brings to their hidden wounds."

This revelation reshaped everything.

And so, with purpose settling like dawn over a long night, I began to ask a question that would change the entire trajectory of my life: *What would it look like to build a space where no one had to suffer alone?* The answer had actually been living in my spirit long before the grief found me.

I trace it all the way back to 2021 — a quiet evening in Ghana, in the warm dark of a bedroom I shared with my then-husband.

We were mapping futures together. I was bouncing an idea off him (something I had carried in my chest for years without yet knowing what to do with it), a mental health private practice unlike any that existed, a space that would see women the way God sees them, not as their wounds, but as their worth. Not as their diagnosis, but as their destiny. I imagined a place where a woman could sit in a therapy chair and in a stylist's chair in the same afternoon. Where lashes and healing, nails and nervous systems, massage and mental health could share the same sacred square footage. I had watched for years how freely women pour their hearts out to stylists and nail technicians (the informal therapists of our culture), and I had always thought: *what if that impulse met trained, intentional care?*

And so, I asked my husband, what we might call such a place. And before I had finished the sentence, the Lord dropped a name into my spirit, quiet and certain as a key turning in a lock: *Beauty in Healing.*

At the time, I believed I understood what those words meant. I was wrong — or rather, I was only seeing the first layer of a much deeper truth. Because the season that followed would teach me that *Beauty in Healing* was never only about a business. It was a prophecy. The trials I endured, the loss that hollowed me out and then slowly, tenderly filled me back up; they were the real curriculum. They stripped the concept of its original meaning and returned it to me transformed, richer and more aching and more alive: *you can find beauty in the very act of healing.* Even from your darkest place. Especially from your darkest place.

The name had been given in 2021. But I did not file the LLC until January of 2023. Almost three years, during which I told myself the timing wasn't right, the resources weren't ready, the season wasn't favorable. I had become fluent in the language of delay; refined, spiritual-sounding excuses that were, in truth, simply fear wearing the clothing of wisdom.

I was an introvert being asked to become visible. I was a private person being asked to share a story I hadn't finished living. I was someone who had spent years pouring into others, now being asked to stand in front of the world and say: *I have something for you.* That terrifies a certain kind of person. It terrified me. What if people didn't agree? What if my grief made me look broken rather than qualified? "What if I shared my story and it wasn't enough? What if I opened up and no one received it?

What finally moved me past the fear was not courage in the dramatic sense. It was grief's quiet dismantling of the illusion that I had unlimited time. Loss has a way of doing that — it strips tomorrow of its assumed certainty, and suddenly the thing you have been postponing until the right conditions arrive reveals itself for what it always was: obedience deferred. God was not waiting for my conditions to be right. He was waiting for me to take the first step so He could give me the next part of the blueprint.

So, I filed the LLC. And I exhaled: the long, shaky exhale of someone who has finally done the thing they were always supposed to do. It felt like obedience. It felt like opening a door the Lord had been standing outside of, knocking for years.

I did not see my first client until November of 2024. The time between was preparation: getting on insurance panels, building the infrastructure, allowing the vision to take its proper shape. And when that first client arrived, I felt what I can only describe as divine confirmation, the sense that this person had not found me by accident, that the Lord had sent them specifically, that my prayer for purpose-aligned souls was already being answered.

I prayed specifically that the Lord would bring me the people He had divinely assigned to me, and I knew from the first conversation that this person was one of them. That is a prayer I still pray every single day. I do not want a full practice built on luck or marketing. I want every person who finds their way to *Beauty in Healing* to have been sent.

*Beauty in Healing* was never just about services. It never had been. The Lord had known all along, and perhaps I had always known somewhere beneath the surface, that the true vision was this: that even in the darkest valley, even in the most suffocating grief, even when you cannot find the floor beneath you, there is beauty to be found. Not beauty that pretends the pain is not real. Not beauty that arrives after the pain has passed. But beauty that *lives inside the healing itself*… available to anyone willing to let God walk them through.

*Beauty in Healing* is also a ministry, the very outpouring of "the Spirit of the Sovereign Lord" upon me, anointing me "to bind up the brokenhearted." Forged in the fire of my own heartbreaks and graces, born out of the most painful season of my life, carried through three years of fear and delay and grief, and finally brought into the light in the middle of my healing. It's the sacred charge the Lord placed in my hands, a haven for every soul who has ever felt too much or too little, too fractured for mending. For outliers and survivors, dreamers whose visions dimmed in the storm… this is sanctuary. Here, you are seen in your fullness, heard without hurry, validated beyond words. And from that holy ground, you walk out equipped, not merely enduring, but thriving through tempests that once threatened to swallow you whole.

The question I am asked most often, in one form or another, is: *What exactly is Beauty in Healing?* Is it counseling? Coaching? Consulting? Mentoring?

The honest answer is yes. All of it. And whatever the sacred moment requires.

As I built *Beauty in Healing*, the Lord made clear who it was for. Not in a boardroom strategy or a marketing plan but in the quiet accumulation of faces, stories, and silent aches that kept finding their way to me. Over time, a portrait formed, and she looked remarkably familiar:

She is a woman. A woman who carries the world with remarkable, exhausting grace. She is a daughter, a mother, a wife, a friend, a sister, a co-worker, a director, a therapist, a minister, a deacon – sometimes all of these at once, sometimes on the same Tuesday afternoon. Her identity has been built almost entirely from what she does for others, from the titles the world assigned her before she ever had the chance to ask herself who she truly was apart from them. She endures enormously. She gives constantly. And somewhere beneath the weight of all she carries, she is quietly losing the thread of her own name.

She may be wrestling with depression that arrived without announcement, or anxiety that settled in her chest like an uninvited tenant. She may be navigating grief that no one around her seems to have the patience for anymore, or the kind of chronic stress that the world now mistakes for ambition. Her self-worth may be fraying at the edges in ways she hasn't yet found the words for. She comes to me not because she was falling apart, but because she was exhausted from pretending, she wasn't.

For those standing at a career crossroads, unsure of the next step, sensing a shift but unable to yet see where it leads, coaching is one of the ways I show up. For MSW-level social workers in New York just finding their footing in clinical work, I offer supervision and mentorship. Someone once poured into me. I have never forgotten what that kind of investment felt like, and I do not take lightly the chance to do the same for someone else.

These are my people. Divinely assigned, carefully held.

A session with me is not what people sometimes expect. It is not formal in the way institutions can make therapy feel; measured, clocked, transactional. It is a conversation. Unhurried, unguarded, and yet purposeful beneath its ease. Many of my clients ask if we can begin with prayer, inviting the Holy Spirit into the room before any clinical word is spoken. I welcome this always. It reminds us both that we are not alone in the work; that there is a wisdom available in that space far beyond my training or my questions.

I ask a lot of Socratic questions. The kind designed not to give answers but to surface them. To hold up a mirror and ask, gently and honestly, *what do you see?* We trace patterns: the behavioral loops that keep repeating, the thought highways that run without supervision, the attachment wounds shaping how a person loves and communicates and moves through the world. I reflect on what I hear. I give homework: worksheets, reflection prompts, and practical tools, because healing has to be livable. It has to hold up on an ordinary day and inside an impossible family dinner. The most transformative work rarely happens in the hour we share together. It happens after, in the quiet attempts at something new.

There is laughter in those rooms. There are tears, the releasing kind, the clarifying kind. There is insight, sometimes sudden and startling, sometimes slow-building and earned. And always, underneath, a current of hope moving stronger than whatever brought someone through the door. The transformation I witness most consistently is not a single dramatic shift but a quiet, cumulative one: shame replaced with understanding, self-condemnation replaced with grace, a fragile borrowed faith replaced with one that is owned and tested and alive.

The people I work with do not leave with perfect lives. They leave with something better: the tools to inhabit their lives fully, even when the storm has not yet passed. A joy that does not depend on circumstances behaving. The knowledge, cellular and sure, that they can endure and thrive because they are no longer alone in any of it.

Three pillars hold everything I do at Beauty in Healing: clinical excellence, faith integration, and compassionate care. And that is my commitment to the people who trust me with their most tender places.

The first thing I want every person who finds me to know is this: *healing is possible for you*. No matter what the trauma holds, no matter how long the loss has lingered or how devastating the setback feels, growth is attainable. Restoration is real. Pain is never dismissed here; it is acknowledged with full, unhurried weight. But it is never allowed to become the final word on who you are or what your future holds.

Every person who enters this space is met with empathy, cultural humility, and emotional safety, because I believe that shame has stolen enough. It has taken enough years, enough voices, enough courage from people who were already fighting. At *Beauty in Healing,* shame is not reinforced; it is gently, consistently replaced with understanding. The clinical frameworks I work within – CBT, DBT, ACT – are evidence-based and proven, and when a client's faith is part of their story, Christian principles are thoughtfully woven in, not imposed but invited, because I have seen what happens when a person's therapy and their theology are finally allowed to breathe the same air.

Faith is the center of everything I do. Not as an add-on or a preference; as a conviction earned through my own wilderness. I have worked with people who do not yet share my faith, and I hold them with the same care. But I have seen, over more than a decade of this work, that the deepest and most lasting transformation belongs to those whose healing is rooted in Christ, because evidence-based tools, as powerful as they are, need a foundation beneath them to hold. And I have found no sturdier foundation than a relationship with the God who designed the human soul.

When I close my eyes and ask the Lord to show me what *Beauty in Healing* looks like at its fullest (five, ten years from now) what I see is not simply a larger practice. What I see is a movement.

I see multiple locations, yes; physical spaces rooted in communities that need them most, where healing is not a luxury reserved for those with the right insurance or the right zip code. But more than square footage and staff rosters, I see something that cannot be built by strategy alone: a bridge. A wide, sturdy, grace-built bridge between the language of clinical mental health and the language of Christian faith, finally standing in the same landscape without apology.

For too long, those two worlds have been held apart (one in the therapy room, one in the sanctuary) as if a person must choose between seeking God and seeking help. My deepest hope is that *Beauty in Healing* becomes a place, and then a *movement*, that dismantles that false divide entirely. That we make it undeniably clear: your faith and your mental wellness were never in competition. They were always meant to heal you together. I believe God gave us therapy. I believe the overlap between clinical intervention and scriptural wisdom is not accidental; it is intentional, woven in from the beginning.

I want to see that work carried into schools, into churches, into boardrooms and community centers, anywhere human beings are quietly drowning inside systems that celebrate productivity over personhood, output over inner life. We live in a world that applauds exhaustion. That mistakes burnout for ambition. That watches people lose time with their children, their spouses, their own souls, and calls it success. I want *Beauty in Healing* to be a gentle, persistent, prophetic voice against that lie.

And for those who arrive without a relationship with God (perhaps wounded by religion, perhaps simply never introduced to Him), I hope we create a space that is gracious enough for them to feel safe to explore. Not pressured. Not preached at. Simply welcomed into an environment where healing is happening, and something about that healing begins to point them toward the Source of it.

At the center of every ambition I carry for this work is one quiet, non-negotiable desire: to make God pleased. Everything built here is built as unto Him. Every session, every breakthrough, every soul that leaves lighter than they arrived… that is His glory, not mine. And if, in five or ten years, people are not merely surviving their lives but actually *living* them (waking up with purpose, showing up with presence, laughing without guilt) then *Beauty in Healing* will have become exactly what the Lord always intended it to be.

*Beauty in Healing* has a scripture. It has always been Romans 8:28: "*And we know that in all things God works for the good of those who love Him, who have been called according to His purpose.*"

It found me, as the truest scriptures tend to, not in a season of ease but in the middle of the wreckage. I was deep in my own decline, holding the question I suspect most suffering people eventually arrive at: *Why? Why all of this? What could possibly be the purpose of this much pain?*

And the Lord, gentle and precise as ever, pointed me to those words. But He did not let me read them the way I had always read them before.

Most of us hear Romans 8:28 and feel the warmth of a promise that things will resolve the way we hope. That eventually, life will reorganize itself into something that looks like what we wanted. And I understand that reading it in that way is human. And it is not entirely wrong. But the Lord showed me something deeper, something that quietly changed everything: *His definition of good is not our definition of good.*

We hold our idea of *good* like a blueprint and measure every season against it, and when the season doesn't match the blueprint, we assume the promise has failed. But the moment I released my blueprint and asked the Lord to show me His, the scripture came alive in a way it never had before. I began to see the ways He had been working; not despite the pain, but *through* it, *in* it, at every turn I had thought I was most alone.

I finally, exhaustedly, loosened my grip on what I had decided His *good* was supposed to look like. I stopped auditing His faithfulness against my comfort. I stopped demanding that the chapter make sense before I would agree to keep reading.

When I turn to look back now, across the full landscape of that season, I see what I could not see while I was inside it. I see that I was never alone. I see *Him,* the Lord, present in every moment I had mistaken for abandonment, holding me in every hour I thought I was simply falling.

He showed me where He had saved me when I didn't know I needed saving. Where He had comforted me in the hours I thought comfort was impossible. Where He had provided, strengthened, directed, and held me at my most fragile – quietly, faithfully, without fanfare. The darkness was real. The pain was real. But so was He, and He had been there for all of it.

I see how He sustained me when my own strength had long since emptied out. I see the comfort that arrived in ways no human hand could have delivered – the unexplainable peace that settled in rooms that had no business being peaceful, the prayers that never found words, only tears, and were somehow, mercifully, still heard. He did not still every wave. But He never once stepped out of the water either.

That is the revelation *Beauty in Healing* was born from. Not that hard things won't come, they will. Not that faith immunizes us from storms, it doesn't. But that when we dare to look back across our hardest seasons through the lens of His definition of *good,* we begin to see something astonishing: those dark, devastating chapters were also, in their own sacred way, *beautiful* because of who we got to discover God to be inside them.

That is what I want for every person who comes through this work. Not just relief from pain, but the encounter with the God that turns even ashes into something quietly, unmistakably beautiful. That encounter changes everything. It changed me. And I have staked everything I am building here on the belief that it can change them, too.

Working with dozens, and over time hundreds, of individuals has humbled me. It reminds me that I am not the source of transformation. I am a participant in it. I witness growth, but I do not manufacture it. I provide skill, structure, and safety, but ultimately it is God who heals, restores, and reshapes hearts.

So, when people ask me how many individuals I have worked with, I sometimes hesitate before answering. Not because I do not know approximately, but because reducing people to numbers feels incomplete. Each person who has sat across from me carried a story that deserved more than arithmetic.

Each client represents hours of sacred conversation. Tears shared in confidential spaces. Breakthroughs that happened slowly and sometimes invisibly. Moments when someone chose vulnerability instead of silence. Moments when shame cracked open just enough for light to enter.

If I am honest, I do not know what the final count will be by the end of my career. I only know that each person who crosses my path matters deeply. Whether fifty or five hundred, each story has shaped me as much as I have shaped them. In many ways, that is what humbles me most: the awareness that what began as my private struggle to rise from my own ashes has quietly become a pathway for others to find their own footing.

# Self-Reflection

1. Where in your life have you been delaying obedience, waiting for "the right time" instead of taking the next step?

______________________________

______________________________

______________________________

______________________________

2. If you truly believed — not just knew, but believed — that your time was not unlimited, what would you stop postponing today?

______________________________

______________________________

______________________________

______________________________

3. In what ways have you defined "good" based on your expectations instead of God's perspective?

______________________________

______________________________

______________________________

______________________________

4. Can you identify moments in your life where God was present, even when you felt abandoned? What do you see now that you didn't see then?

______________________________

______________________________

______________________________

______________________________

5. What would it look like for you to shift from asking "Why is this happening?" to "What can this become?"

6. Are you willing to let your story be used as a bridge for someone else's healing? Why or why not?

7. If your life is an assignment, what do you sense you've been entrusted to carry, build, or release into the world?

***Want to go deeper with your reflection?*** *After you complete this chapter's journal prompts, you can choose to share your answers privately with me. With your consent, your story may be included anonymously in a future devotional sequel.*

..... / .... / ......
S M T W T F S

*Still have more to say?*
*This space is yours. Keep going.*

SPEAK THIS OVER YOURSELF

# Nothing in my story is wasted. Nothing in my pain is random. God is not absent in my struggle. He is active in my becoming.

***Heavenly Father,***

*I confess that I have measured Your goodness by my comfort. I have defined "good" by ease, relief, and restored normalcy. But today, I lay down my expectations. If You are forming me in this fire, then give me strength to endure it. If You are shaping something deeper than I can see, help me trust the process. Redeem what I thought was wasted. Anchor me when the waves rise. Remind me that presence is greater than preference. Turn my ashes into assignment. And turn my survival into testimony.* ***In Jesus' name, Amen.***

*#Scan2Rise*

# scan to *Rise!*

*Scan the QR Code to book a private session with me. I would be honored to walk with you.*

*Let this be the step where you choose healing.*

# IX

# RISE, HE'S CALLING YOU

*"So, Jesus stood still and commanded him to be called. Then they called the blind man, saying to him, "Be of good cheer. Rise, He is calling you."*
*– Mark 10:49*

If you have lingered with me until this moment, I want to pause and simply acknowledge your presence. You have walked through the ashes with me, step by step. You have stood in the echoing silence of hospital rooms, shared the ache of unanswered prayers as they hung, trembling, in the waiting air. In these pages, we have been honest about fear, the kind of fear that creeps into the corners, braiding itself through plans and dreams, threatening to rewrite the stories we hold dear.

As you turned these pages, maybe something deep within you was stirred. Perhaps you glimpsed yourself in my questions, those whispered doubts and desperate hopes. Maybe you revisited fresh wounds, or the scars you thought time had faded. Maybe you simply felt tired—bone-deep tired—of carrying burdens that were never yours to bear alone.

Years ago, Ray Boltz sang words that I heard in passing: "That's what this altar is for. You don't have to carry those burdens anymore."

This altar is not a physical one with polished wood and stained glass behind it, but the kind that exists in the unseen space between surrender and trust. The place where you stop negotiating with God and start placing the full weight of your humanity into His hands.

The altar is not about religion or ritual. It is not about proving your worthiness or composing yourself before heaven. It is a place of sacred exchange. It is where fear is handed over and peace begins to settle. Where shame is laid down and mercy answers back. Where exhaustion meets grace strong enough to hold it.

At this altar, I have learned to lay down my ashes, my disappointments, my brokenness, the residue of sorrow that clings to all of us. And in return, what I find is beauty. I have brought fear like a tattered cloak, and received peace more honest and steadier than anything I could muster on my own. My story, once fragmented by loss and longing, is finding redemption word by word, page by page, grace by grace, day by day. Every jagged line, every shattered hope, is being rewritten as part of something more beautiful and whole than I ever dared imagine.

The old-rugged cross is still standing, a cross that remains unmovable even when all else shifts beneath our feet. To me, it is the place where shame is silenced, where guilt and sickness and even death are forced to bow. This is where my story met its truest turning point. In a stark hospital room, when I reached the end of myself, I wasn't alone. The same gentle presence that steadied my shaking hands, breathed peace into my panic, and whispered hope when everything within me screamed despair. That presence can meet you now, wherever you are.

Jesus is waiting. He is calling you, too. Not when you have "figured it all out." Not when you become perfect or untarnished. Not tomorrow, or next week, or in some imagined future where your life finally lines up. The invitation is for you, now, in all the mess and beauty of your heart, your history, your hopes.

It's an open invitation sealed with love that won't let go. An invitation to step out of self-reliance and into surrender. "Come to the altar," the invitation hums, "the Father's arms are open wide." If you feel that quiet pull (a gentle nudge within your chest), pause and listen. That's not a coincidence. It's not your imagination. That's the Savior asking you to come rest in his everlasting, ever-loving arms. That's Love itself, stretching out its hand toward you, whispering you are not alone, you do not have to do this alone anymore. The altar is for you. It is for all of us, no exceptions.

Maybe you've known about Jesus for years. Maybe his name was a song you heard in childhood or a whisper you tried to forget. Maybe you walked away when life became complicated, or maybe you've just been wandering, holding your story close in silent ache.

Today can be different.

If today you're ready—really ready—to lay everything down, to surrender your life to Jesus, fully and sincerely, you can pray from wherever you are right now because surrender spoken aloud becomes real in the heart:

*Lord Jesus,*

*I come to You just as I am.*

*With my ashes.*
*With my mistakes.*

*With the parts of my story, I have tried to hide.*

*I believe You died on the Cross for my sins.*
*I believe You rose again.*

*Today, I surrender to You.*
*Be my Lord. Be my Savior.*
*Be my Restorer.*
*Be my Healer.*

*Forgive me.*
*Wash me clean.*
*Make me new.*

*I choose to follow You.*

*From this day forward.*
*No turning back.*

*In Jesus' name,*
*Amen.*

You said yes. Heaven rejoices. You have risen. I'd love to celebrate you. Share your salvation story or testimony with me. Scan the QR code or email: *Jesus@iambrittanyjenkins.com*

SPEAK THIS OVER YOURSELF

# I'm not what tried to break me. I'm not what I lost. I am redeemed By the Blood of Jesus. And this is where I rise.

***Father,***

*Thank You for this soul who has said yes to Jesus. Seal this decision in their heart. Root them deeply in Christ. Strengthen them when they are weak. Guard their mind and steady their steps. Keep them faithful and strong until Your coming. Let their life shine as a testimony of grace. In Jesus' mighty name, Amen.*

**Welcome to your New Beginning!**

# X
# EPILOGUE

I didn't write this book because I conquered every fire. No, I wrote it because I discovered God sitting with me in the smoke; right there, close enough to feel His breath.

And if my story has stirred something in you, I pray it's given you permission to grieve honestly, to question without shame, to hope again even when it feels foolish. I pray it has reminded you that ashes are evidence of what once blazed; proof of a life fiercely lived and loved, deeply cherished, now spent. What lingers may seem shapeless, hollowed out, shrouded in shadow. But that chaos? God knows it well. Recall Genesis: the earth formless and void, darkness thick over the deep, and the Spirit hovering, poised to speak light into nothing. It was into that formlessness that God spoke light. It was from that emptiness that life emerged. What if your ashes herald not an ending, but the dawn of re-creation?

If you're holding this book with your own ashes still clinging. Smelling of smoke. Heavy on your skin. Hear this softly: you're not late to healing. Questions don't brand you faithless. The weight you carry isn't failure. The ache's persistence doesn't mean defeat.

Rising seldom thunders.

It mirrors Naaman at the Jordan, plunging seven times into muddy waters, each dip yielding no fanfare. Picture the pause after the third: obedience teetering on absurdity, healing a distant mirage. Yet beneath the surface, unseen, renewal gathered force. The Jordan has ever been a threshold—shedding old skins, birthing new names. Baptism's echo: surrender the sunk cost of yesterday, emerge into tomorrow's promise. So rising often quickens long before your eyes perceive it—ignited the instant surrender eclipses despair.

Rising is like Naaman in the muddy Jordan, dipping seven times while nothing changed after three, four, five, six. His Obedience felt foolish. His healing seemed a long way off. Yet, in that humble act of going down one more time, restoration took place.

Rising can feel like that.

It can feel unseen. It can seem like you are sinking beneath the weight of grief, doubt, or disappointment with no sign of change. But something is happening beneath what you can see. The Jordan, after all, has always been a place of crossing; a place to leave old identities behind and start new ones. It is the kind of water that reminds us of baptism, of letting go of what was and rising into what will be. And so rising, sometimes, begins long before your skin looks different; it starts the moment you choose surrender over despair.

As you set this book down, I won't pray for a pain-free road ahead. That won't be honest. Instead:

May the ashes that marked your grief become the soil for your growth. May you find God in the places where you once felt abandoned.

May you discover courage in the situations where you feel weak. May peace guard your heart when uncertainty whispers. May you sense God's presence in rooms that once echoed with fear.

May your story, including the parts you wish didn't happen, open the door for someone else's healing. May the challenges you faced lead you to a stronger version of yourself.

And when you forget, as we all do, may the grace of God gently remind you that your story is still being written; that your beauty is emerging from places you once saw as ruined.

You see, this story doesn't end here.

Not mine. Not yours.

Your pain is a plan...

Rise!

# Final-Reflection

**1. What are the ashes in your story?**

*Name them honestly. Loss. Fear. Betrayal. Delay. Diagnosis. Disappointment. Write them down without minimizing them.*

**2. What did those seasons try to convince you about yourself?**

*Did they whisper that you were not enough? Unworthy? Forgotten? Replace those lies with truth.*

**3. Where did you survive when you thought you wouldn't?**

*Identify moments where you kept going — even when you were exhausted. That is evidence of strength.*

**4. What has pain taught you about your capacity?**

*What resilience, wisdom, boundaries, or faith were formed in the fire?*

**5. What does "rising" look like for you now?**

*Not someday. Not perfectly. But in this season. Is it forgiving? Starting over? Seeking help? Resting? Dreaming again? What?*

**6. What new belief will you carry forward?**

*Finish this sentence*

*I am no longer:* ____________________

*I am becoming:* ____________________

**7. If your life were a testimony, what would the title be?**

*Give your story a redemptive name.*

____________________

____________________

**8. What are you ready to release?**

*Write a goodbye letter to the version of you who carried unnecessary shame, guilt, or blame.*

____________________

____________________

____________________

____________________

____________________

____________________

____________________

____________________

____________________

____________________

____________________

*Sign:* ____________ *Date:* ____________

# ABOUT THE AUTHOR

Brittany Jenkins does not arrive at the end of this memoir as a woman who has conquered her pain; she arrives as one who has been *changed* by it. Her story is at once achingly human and quietly extraordinary: a life shaped by grief, illness, and faith, and by the stubborn belief that none of it goes to waste.

By profession, Brittany is a licensed clinical social worker and the founder of *Beauty in Healing, LLC,* a mental health practice rooted in the conviction that wholeness is not only possible – it is promised. Her work with clients, particularly women navigating loss, diagnosis, and the disorienting work of rebuilding, flows directly from the terrain she has walked herself.

At twenty-nine, Brittany's world shifted without warning when an incurable blood disorder entered her story, dismantling the identity she had built as a self-reliant athlete. She would go on to find love, marry, and build a life; only to face a grief of an entirely different kind when, just two years into her marriage, she lost her husband. It was in the weight of these, and the many others these pages have already borne witness to, that she made a covenant with herself in those long, sleepless nights: if healing came, she would share the road that led her there.

What distinguishes Brittany is not merely what she has endured – it is how she has endured it. She does not preach resilience as a hardening of the spirit. She teaches it as a *softening* – a willingness to release what cannot be controlled, to let faith carry what strength cannot. Her motto, "*Nothing wasted,*" is not a bumper sticker sentiment; it is a theology lived out in real time, anchored in Romans 8:28 and tested in seasons most people would not choose.

As a speaker, Brittany addresses audiences with the kind of empathy that can only be earned. She speaks to the grieving spouse, the newly diagnosed, the person quietly relearning how to exist inside a life that no longer looks familiar. Her presence in a room – much like her presence on these pages – functions as a steady reminder: *you are not alone, and this is not the end.*

Beyond the book, her influence continues in the social workers she mentors, the clients she guides, and the community she is actively building around mental health, faith, and healing. She is not a woman defined by her accolades, though they are many. She is defined, in her own words, by one practice: waking up each morning and choosing trust — in the storm and in the sun alike.

Brittany Jenkins is, above all else, a witness. A witness to suffering that did not destroy her, to a God she calls *El Roi,* the One who sees, and to the quietly radical truth that beauty and brokenness are not opposites. They are, in her life and in this memoir, inseparable companions on the road toward grace.

She is still on that road. Still rising. Still surrendering. And by every measure that matters, still becoming.

# brittany jenkins

Author,
Social Worker,
Therapist.

*Working with Brittany has helped me build my confidence and regain a sense of purpose in life. She's helped me to learn so much about my mental health but how to use my faith as well. I am not able to navigate the world and interpersonal relationships more confidently.*

*– Sofia Reyes*

*Brittany has been one of the best therapists I've worked with. I was dealing with complex grief and trauma when I found her and she helped me navigate that challenging time with compassion, faith, and clinical expertise. The tools that she's provided and the encouragement through prayer have been exactly what I needed to get through.*

*– Danielle Moore*

*Without a doubt, I have the best counselor in the world! Brittany is truly phenomenal. She's empathetic, insightful, and not afraid to challenge you when it's needed... Her Christian counseling has been life-changing, helping me manage anxiety through practical coping techniques while encouraging me to grow stronger in prayer and faith... Every time I leave a session, I feel lighter, like a weight has been lifted. I'm always reminded that there's hope, even for things that feel unattainable... I am so grateful that my prayer was answered in my search for a Godly and knowledgeable therapist.*

*– Paige Bennett*

*Before working with you, I felt overwhelmed and unsure of how to fully process my thoughts and emotions. I am experiencing compound grief and did not know how to fully process any of it. Through our work together, I am gaining clarity about myself and have begun to understand my patterns in a deeper, more intentional way. You created a safe, supportive space that allowed me to be honest and actually do the work. I've learned how to respond with intention instead of reacting out of habit, and that shift has been powerful. To anyone considering Beauty in Healing, I would say this is real healing work, grounding, empowering, and truly transformative.*

*– Keisha Williams*

***Names have been changed to protect the confidentiality of our clients.***

*Kindly leave me a*

# *Review*

*Scan the QR code to leave a review on Google.*

*If this book met you in your ashes. If it reminded you that healing is possible. If it helped you rise... Would you share that?*

APPENDIX

# PLAYLIST THAT HELD ME

These songs were *ministry.*

They filled my room on the mornings I could not get up. They were on repeat during the hours I spent with just the Lord, shut in from the world, learning – really learning – what it meant to trust Him with something I could not fix.

Some of these songs made me cry. Some made me lift my hands even when my heart felt heavy. Some reminded me that God was still near when nothing around me confirmed it.

This playlist is a record of how the Lord sustained me. Let them carry you the way they carried me. Scan the QR code on the next page to access the playlist.

And as you listen, know this: the same God who held me in those quiet, uncertain moments is holding you right now too. He never stopped being near. No. Not once.

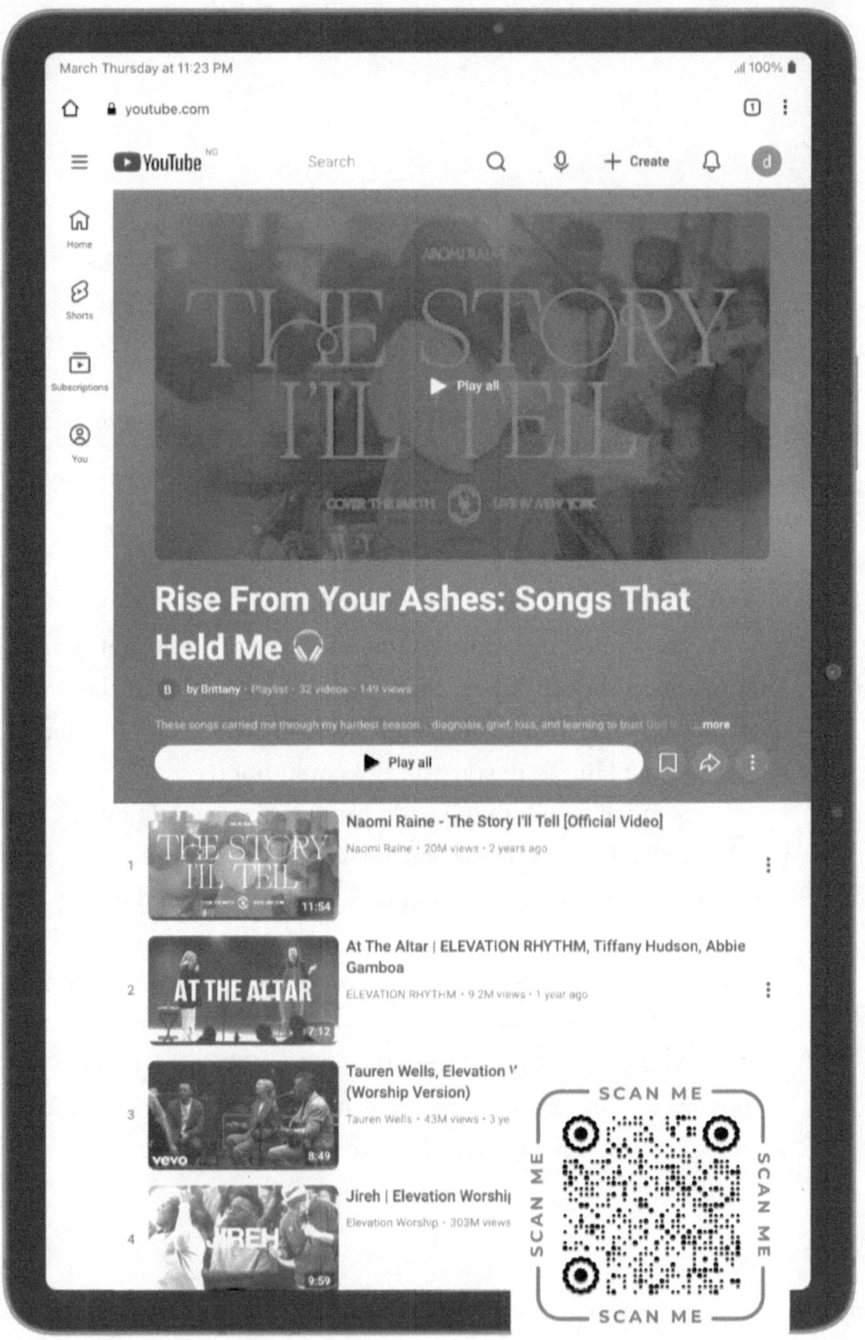
March Thursday at 11:23 PM
100%
youtube.com
YouTube
Search
Create
Home
Shorts
Subscriptions
You
THE STORY I'LL TELL
Play all
Rise From Your Ashes: Songs That Held Me
by Brittany · Playlist · 32 videos · 149 views
Play all
Naomi Raine - The Story I'll Tell [Official Video]
Naomi Raine · 20M views · 2 years ago
11:54
At The Altar | ELEVATION RHYTHM, Tiffany Hudson, Abbie Gamboa
ELEVATION RHYTHM · 9.2M views · 1 year ago
AT THE ALTAR
7:12
(Worship Version)
Tauren Wells · 43M views
vevo
8:49
Jireh | Elevation Worship
Elevation Worship · 303M views
JIREH
9:59
SCAN ME

## NOTE OF THANKS

First and foremost, all glory belongs to God. Every page of this book is evidence of His grace, His mercy, and His steadfast love for me.

I also want to acknowledge the many people, organizations, groups, communities, and churches the Lord placed along this journey. Some for a season. Some for a lifetime, and some in quiet, behind-the-scenes ways they may never fully realize. A phone call at the right moment. A meal left at the door. A prayer whispered on my behalf in a room I never entered. I saw it. I felt it. And I have not forgotten.

Some were in the room. Some walked beside me. Some showed up through a screen, across miles and time zones, and it mattered just the same. Some were a phone call away. Some spoke life into me directly. Some never knew my name, and some simply sang, and in their singing, God used them to carry me when I could not carry myself. Their worship became the soundtrack of my healing.

I have listed your names here alphabetically, because in my heart, every single one of you holds an equal and irreplaceable place. There is no hierarchy in gratitude this deep.

Abbie Gamboa,
Anthny,
CalledOut Music,
Chandler Moore,
Deb Orah,
Efua B,
Elevation Rhythm,
Elevation Worship,
Grace Tena,
Lakeview Community,
Lauren Adebayo *(the mutual friend that introduced me to Eric and sacrificed time to read scripture with me after he passed)*
Lord Sarfo *(Eric's Father),*
Malverne Community,
Margaret Sarfo *(Eric's Mother),*
Marizu,
Maverick City,
Michael Oyo,
Micheal Bethany,
Naomi Raine,
New Life Christian Center *(my childhood church),*
Ore Macaulay,
Pastor Butler,
Pastor Katherine Corbett,
Samira *(Eric's childhood friend),*
Shana Wilson-Williams,
Sinmidele,
Tauren Wells,
Tiffany Hudson,
Todd Dulaney
Victor Thompson,
West Hempstead Community.

You are all woven into this work in ways words cannot fully capture. And I pray that God honors every seed you have sown – knowingly or unknowingly – in ways that far exceed anything you could ask or imagine.

*With a grateful heart,*
**Brittany Jenkins**

#BEAUTYINHEALING

# Connect with us!

**TikTok**
*@beautyinhealing*

**Instagram**
*@_britt_any_j*

**YouTube**
*@beautyinhealingtv*

*Thank You*

www.ingramcontent.com/pod-product-compliance
Lightning Source LLC
LaVergne TN
LVHW090516110826
845146LV00003B/883

* 9 7 9 8 9 9 5 4 4 5 4 0 1 *